Clay for All Seasons:

Helen Cruickshank

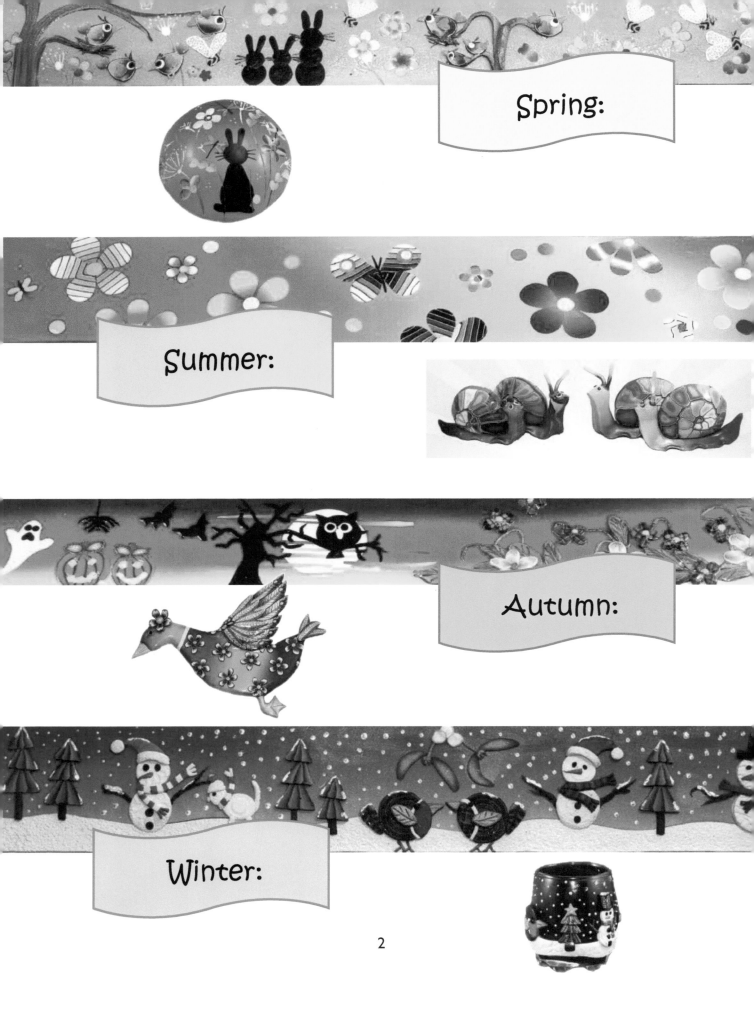

Spring:

Summer:

Autumn:

Winter:

2

Clay for all Seasons:

Blue Seabird Clay Designs

13 Projects:

23 Cane designs:

Step-by--step Instructions:

Helen Cruickshank.

First published 2021   Blue Seabird Clay Designs
helen.cruickshank@blueseabirdclaydesigns.co.uk   Website: www.blueseabirdclaydesigns.com

Every effort has been made to ensure that all information in this book is accurate. However, due to differing conditions, tools, and individual skills, the publisher cannot be responsible for any injuries, losses, or other damages that may result from the use of the information in this book.

While polymer clay is branded as non-toxic and safe when used correctly, it is advisable to follow certain guidelines: do not eat it, do not let baked or unbaked polymer clay come in contact with food, wash your hands after using polymer clay, use clay-dedicated tools, avoid burning polymer clay by following the clay manufacturers' recommended baking temperatures and times, and supervise children who are using polymer clay. Use extreme caution when working with any tools with sharp edges or points, such as the tissue blades or needle tools, to avoid injury. Always supervise children who used sharp tools.

ISBN : 978-1-7398582-0-9

This book is dedicated to
my friend Donna Baratta.

For always giving me unstinting support.

For challenging me and helping me look at my designs
in different ways.

For being the absolute best type of friend,

and a wonderful clayer.

Acknowledgements:

I love my clay, and I'm very lucky to have a husband who allows me to fill a part of our lounge with a clay area and many many shelves for all the clay paraphanalia which I just 'have' to buy. He also doesn't object when we watch a film together and I'm claying, so constantly ask questions such as "who's that person" and "what's just happened?". In case I don't say it much, I do appreciate you Iain! The rest of the family is supportive as well, my sister Ruth helps me make the Christmas cat decorations for the cat charity each year, and mum buys them! Dad tells me that my flying ducks are the most naff thing he's ever seen so gives me hours of fun telling him he's getting a set for Christmas. My daughter supports me and is always happy to talk about colour, and my nephew Jack oohs and aahs over things, and as he's very creative himself is always nice to hear.

My friend Linda has done stirling work helping me get the 100 cats made each year for the charity, and I'm often inviting her over for supper, very thinly disguised as an evening in the cat making sweat shop! This year I roped in her friend Belinda as well, and our friend Audrey, so we might aim for 200 next year.

However, there are two people who help me progress in my clay and the more business side of it. Donna Barratta is my friend in America who I met in France at a polymer clay workshop (of course) and we've become firm friends. We used to travel each year to see each other, but since the pandemic have started using zoom to meet and clay together. Donna has a wonderful sense of colour and style and is meticulous in her work, which contrasts brilliantly with my slightly less great skills in colour and style, and faster pace of working. We give each other ideas, help each other see things differently, and offer constructive criticism which is helpful and needed in order to grow. She's also incredibly supportive of all I do in clay, and the first person I share any new ideas with.

The other person is Penny Vingoe of Clayaround. Penny I also met at a polymer clay workshop and again have become firm friends with. Penny runs the wonderful Clayaround which provides us British with clay and everything that goes with it! She's an incredible source of knowledge of who's who in the clay world, what's new, and who's running what workshop. She's also a businesswoman, which I am definitely not, and pushes me to look beyond just playing with clay, into making it something more; a goal I have but lack the oomph to get there. She challenges me, cadjouls me, and encourages me, and is always there to bounce ideas off. She and Donna are the two people that I look forward to sharing my ideas with, and know they wont glaze over!

I have so many friends in the clay world, all who offer me encouragement and are incredibly nice about my work. My Irish friends are a wonderful bunch and I'm looking forward to travelling over to Ireland again next year for more laughs and clay. The tutors that I've attended workshops with are always supportive and very generous with their advice, and learning more techniques is always with a view to adding them somehow into an animal!

All in all I'm very lucky to have the support of family and friends, a place to clay, and a job that allows me to buy the clay! I said I won't do any more books after this one, but I've already got a few ideas...........

Introduction:

I can't quite believe I'm writing a second book!

I'm still working as an Occupational Therapist in Mental Health, and while I was writing this book the Covid-19 pandemic hit the world. I found out that not only did this impact on people's mental and physical health, but it also impacted on my ability to be creative. Creativity is the ability to express oneself freely, without anxiety or inhibition, and this was difficult when the world was reeling from disaster and struggling.
However, life started to return to a different type of normality and I decided that this book needed to be written.

Since my last book I've focussed on continuing to learn as many different techniques as I could find. I've had some wonderful weekends in Rome, Bristol and Ireland, learning from wonderful tutors, surrounded by other clay enthusiasts, and going home full of enthusiam and motivation. One positive thing to come out of the pandemic is the development of learning by virtual means, and I've been able to attend workshops with people such as Sarah Shriver and Bettina Welker who I would never have been able to travel to in the past. I've also had the opportunity to run workshops myself, something that I love and hope to develop further in the future, not only in person, but latterly by zoom.

This book is essentially a book of tutorials; I tried making it more 'designy', but I'm not a professional book designer, and I felt that I needed to make sure that it was a book that anyone could follow and actually achieve the projects in it, rather than a book that only looked good on a coffee table. It's not perfect; every time I look at it I see titles that aren't perfectly centred, photos that I could have done better, and various other imperfections, but I loved designing and making the projects, and can't wait to share them with others, so decided to take courage, and write it.

I found this quote by Ray Bradbury

> "You've got to jump off cliffs and build your wings on the way down"

So I jumped, and hope my wings develop on the way down.

Contents:

8

Pasta Machine settings:

There are many different pasta machine used for polymer clay, and all have different thicknesses. Not only that, but some machines have the lowest numbers as the thickest settings, and the higher numbers the thinnest, and others have completely the opposite, some have 9 settings, some 7, and so on.

PM3

Therefore, instead of giving instructions such as 'the thickest setting on your pasta machine', I've measured the thickness of each of my Atlas Pasta Machine settings using standard playing cards in order for you to know what thickness I'm using throughout the tutorials.

I've abrieviated each setting to PM0 - 9. PM standing for Pasta Machine, and the number is the setting number. So, PM3 is pasta machine setting 3.

PM0

My pasta machine thicknesses for each setting:
PM0 = 8 standard playing cards
PM1 = 7 standard playing cards
PM2 = 6 standard playing cards
PM3 = 4 standard playing cards
PM4 = 3 standard playing cards
PM6
PM5 = 2.5 standard playing cards
PM6 = 2 standard playing cards
PM7 = 1 standard playing card
PM8 & 9 = less than 1 standard playing card

To find out the thicknesses of the settings on the pasta machine you're using:

• First put your pasta machine on the thickest setting
• Put a few standard playing cards together and put them through the machine.
• Keep adding cards until you have reached the maximum number that can go through in one pass
• Write this down, then continue for all the settings on your machine
• Then compare your machine thicknesses with mine
• For example: If my PM6 is 2 cards thick, but your PM5 is 2 cards thick, every time you see PM6, you will use

Health and Safety - boring but important information!

CAUTION - SHARP TOOLS:
The instructions in this book include the use of knives, tissue blades, cocktail sticks, needle tools and other sharp instruments. Using sharp tools may result in injury; use with extreme care, keep out of reach of children, and supervise young people.

IS CLAY TOXIC?
Many people are concerned about the toxicity of polymer clay. Ginger Davis Allman of The Blue Bottle Tree wrote an excellent article on the safety of polymer clay, it can be found at https://thebluebottletree.com/polymer-clay-safe/. Safety information by Polyform, who make Sculpey and Premo clay, can also be found at www.sculpey.com.

WHAT IS POLYMER CLAY?

Polymer Clay is a synthetic modelling material that remains flexible until it is cured by baking at a low temperature in a normal oven. It doesn't dry out at room temperature, is made from a basis of PVC resin and a liquid plasticizer, and can be shaped and re-shaped without deterioration. It is perfect for everyone, from beginners to professional artists, and there really is no limit to the designs and projects you can make with it.   The only limit is your

Different types of clay:

There are several types of polymer clay, but the one I use most, and throughout this book, is Premo Sculpey.   In a nutshell, this is a synopsis of, in my opinion, some of the most easily available clays:

- **Fimo Professional** (85g/3oz & 350g/12.34oz blocks)
  exceptionally versatile clay, strong when cured, suitable for all
  projects especially cane work.
  The only drawback is that it takes longer to condition. One of my favourite clays for canes.

- **Fimo Soft** - (57g/2oz blocks) soft and easy to condition and use, ideal for children and modelling but far too soft for cane making. This is the clay that's the most easy to buy in craft shops.

- **Fimo Effects** (57g/2oz blocks) - comes in different effects eg pearl, nightglow (florescent), glitter, translucent, stone, metallic, pastel & gemstone. Great to use on their own or mixed with other clay.

- **Premo Sculpey** (56g/2oz, 227g/8oz & 454g/1lb blocks) - fantastic range of colours, the larger size blocks are in selected colours only. This is my favourite clay, it's easy to condition but can be too soft for caning if fresh, however, if you leach it (put sheets of clay between paper to 'leech' some of the oil out of the clay) there are no problems. Good for all projects.

- **Premo Sculpey Accents** (57g/2oz & 454g/1lb blocks) - similar to Premo Sculpey and used the same way. Many colours with pearlised, metallic, translucent, granite and glitter effects. Great to use alone or mixed with other clay. I use them a lot throughout this book.

- **Kato Polyclay** (57g/2oz, 354g/12.5oz, and 4 x 1oz blocks in a pack) - this is a wonderful clay for canes, the best I've found. The drawbacks are that it's slightly more expensive, takes longer to condition and has a strong plastic smell which people either seem to love or hate - I love it! It is cured at a slightly higher temperature to Fimo and Premo and if I want to make a complicated cane, I always use Kato

- **Cernit** (56g and 500g blocks) - many colours in wonderful categories eg Glamour, Nature, Neon and Doll. I love the new metallic range, wonderful for mica shift. I don't use it for caning, but if fresh it just needs leaching then it is fine.   Wonderful for modelling, look up Karen Walker and see what she creates with Cernit.   11

Conditioning Polymer Clay:

Polymer clay is easier to use if conditioned (thoroughly mixed) prior to use. It used to be believed that unconditioned clay, even if it appears soft, does not have properly aligned particles and can be less strong, more brittle and break more easily once cured. However, since I wrote my first book the thoughts about this have changed, and a wonderful article in The Blue Bottle Tree explains why the only reason to condition clay is to make it easier to work with. I still always condition clay before using as it doesn't crack and is much easier to use, so whether the old or the new thinking is right, you won't go wrong by conditioning it. There are two ways to do this, either with your hands or a pasta machine.

1. To use your hands, cut off some clay from the block and roll it between your hands into a ball shape. Next roll it into a long snake or log shape, then back into a ball. Repeat this until the clay doesn't crack or split when you fold it in half.

2. To condition using a pasta machine, cut your block of clay into thin slices, then put through the pasta machine on the thickest setting. Put two of the slices together and put through the pasta machine again. Fold the clay sheet in half and put through the pasta machine again, with the folded side going through the machine first. Repeat until the clay is pliable and does not crack or split when folded.

Curing your clay pieces:

You will need either your normal oven to cure the clay in, or a separate one if you prefer to keep clay and food separate. I bought a small one for £25 and it works well, although I use my normal oven for larger items such as the llama or flat cow. It is really important that you buy an oven thermometer and use it all the time. Small ovens in particular tend to 'spike', ie the temperature goes high very quickly, so always pre-heat your oven for around 20 minutes, and wait until the temperature levels out before putting your clay items in.

How I cure my clay.

- Pre-heat the oven to the clay manufacturers recommended temperature, although for Premo I always cure at 130°C. Wait until the temperature is stable - around 20 minutes
- Place your clay item on a tile and put the tile in an aluminium foil tray. To avoid your clay becoming shiny where it touches the tile, cover the tile with paper.
- Use another foil tray, or a sheet of foil, to cover the clay - this stops the oven's heating element from burning the clay. Alternatively you can put the clay in the oven and cover loosely with foil. It's not essential to cover your clay, I often don't bother, but for important pieces I don't take chances and cover them
- Instead of the tile, I often cure many of my pieces by filling the tray with cornflower and putting my pieces in it - this stops things rolling away or getting flat and shiny from the tile.

The basic clay kit:

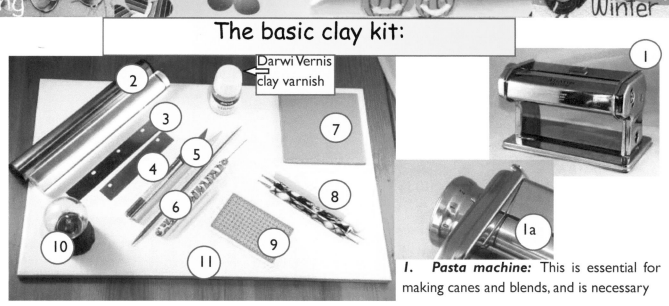

Darwi Vernis clay varnish

1.   **Pasta machine:** This is essential for making canes and blends, and is necessary for every project in the book. I have an Atlas Wellbeing 180 which I love, but you don't need an expensive one. Two rollers in the pasta machine squeeze the clay to a sheet of a determined width; the width is adjusted by turning a round gauge on the side (1a).

2.   **Acrylic or metal roller:** For flattening and smoothing the clay, especially before putting through the pasta machine, when lengthening square canes, and smoothing surfaces.

3.   **Clay blades - flexible and rigid:** The flexible blades (often called tissue blades) tend to be sharper than the rigid ones and are used mostly to cut thin slices from canes. The rigid blades are useful when you need to make a straight cut in a cane, without distorting.

4.   **Craft knife:** This little knife has lots of uses; cutting round templates and trimming edges etc

5.   **Pointed tools:** I use various sized knitting needles and cable needles, the larger needles are useful to smooth uneven clay, and the smaller ones have numerous uses.

6.   **Needle tool:** When you buy this it has a wood or metal handle, I just covered mine with clay. This has many uses, including making holes and texturing.

7.   **Small tile**: I buy these from a large DIY shop and they cost around 20p each. Useful for putting individual projects on to work on, then later cure on.

8.   **Ball tools of various sizes:** Used to put round indentations in clay. I find many uses for these.

9.   **A standard playing card, or a piece of card 9cm x 6cm:** This is my go-to template for making Skinner blends. As I enjoy making canes so much, I don't like making huge ones, and the playing card is just the right size to make a blend that makes a cane large enough for most of my projects.

10. **A light bulb:** This is not actually essential, but so useful for making curved rounded pieces. Cover the bottom of the bulb with clay to make it stand up, or use a cut off cardboard roll (eg toilet roll) which also works well.

11. **A ceramic tile to work on:** You don't need one as large as the one in the picture.

Other tools and materials:

I use many different shapes and sizes of cutters, but the most useful ones are the circles. Kemper Kutters are my favourite as they have a little plunger to push the clay out if it gets stuck. Other useful shapes are ovals, hearts, stars, squares, flowers and leaves. The three size set of circles, 2cm, 3cm & 4cm are essential in the tool kit, and reasonably inexpensive to buy.

I use a clear glass cutting board with a plastic sheet of quilters grid taped underneath. I've photographed the board with a large white tile underneath so you can see it more clearly. The quilter grid is in square inches but you'll see that on the bottom I've put a line of centimetres so I have both metric and imperial. The pink pattern on the top left is my guide to making a step cane, and the blue straight line is the width of my pasta machine so when I make larger Skinner blends I cut the clay sheet to the right size.

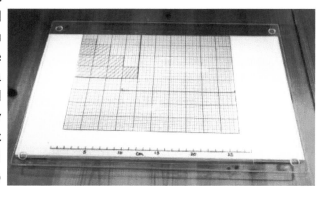

A clay extruder makes long lengths of clay in various shapes. Load clay into the barrel, fix the disc with the hole in the shape of clay you want, turn the handle and voila, lengths of perfectly formed clay! I use it to make clay knitting, canes, edges of pendants, coils, and many other things. Make sure you buy one with a handle, not the very cheap ones that you have to push the clay out manually.

Throughout this book I use Sculpey Bake & Bond clay adhesive, it glues cured clay to non-cured clay. The reason I use the Bake & Bond so often is because many of my projects involve sticking things like cured ears into holes, and the Bake & Bond is liquid, so goes into the holes well. However, my friend Penny Vingoe introduced me to Genesis thick medium extender which is the texture of petrolium jelly (Vaseline) and because it's not a liquid, is very easy to use on flatter pieces. Poly paste, a polymer clay adhesive by Kato is equally as good, so don't feel you have to buy Bake & Bond if you have another clay adhesive.

Often you need to smooth out the surface of your clay, this is called 'burnishing'. To do this lay a piece of thin paper (layout or parchment for example) over your piece and rub something smooth over it. This can be many things, smooth pebble, bone folder, finger etc, but a soapstone (shown left) is inexpensive and perfect for the job.

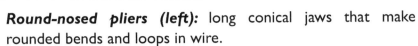

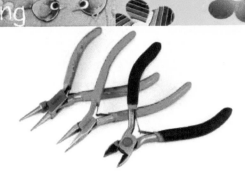

Round-nosed pliers (left): long conical jaws that make rounded bends and loops in wire.

Flat-nosed pliers (middle): flat broad jaws used to grip wire and make sharper bends. I use two pairs in my work as I often grip both ends of a piece of wire and pull to straighten.

Wire cutters (right): as I'm not making jewellery in this book I don't buy expensive wire cutters, anything that will cut 1mm wire.

The Marxit tool is very useful for making evenly spaced marks in clay before cutting slices of equal widths. It has six sides and the marks range from 3mm increments to 20mm. This photo shows my rather grubby but well used Marxit.

Silicone rubber clay shaper tools are useful for making texture in polymer clay and making softer indentations such as in the turtle flippers. They can also be used to smooth over marks in your clay.

A ruler is essential to your polymer clay kit and should have been in the basic clay kit! Make sure you buy a metal one rather than a plastic one as polymer clay can 'melt' certain plastics.

Ultra fine glitter. I sometimes use this on canes when I want to highlight the slices such as on feathers but I also use it to make sheets of shiny clay which can be used in many projects, for example the tree lights and parcel wrapping for the Christmas cats. Make sure you only buy ultra fine glitter as anything larger will result in a grainy surface on your clay.

Gilder's paste can be used to add metallic colour to cured polymer clay. I use various ones, Inca Gold, Pebeo Gilding wax and Creative Expressions Metallic gilding wax. They work particularly well on Steampunk.

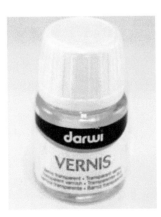

Darwi Vernis - Polymer clay varnish and my varnish of choice as it covers evenly and dries in around 15 minutes. There are other polymer clay varnishes available and it is personal choice.

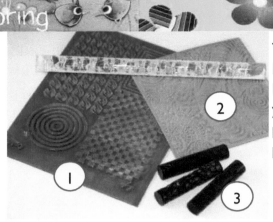

Texture makers. These can be commercial ones such as Helen Breil's (1) and Cernit's (2) texture plates, and the Kor tools (3) and MKM rollers, or you can use items that you probably have round the house such as a toothbrush, pan scrubber, threaded bar, buttons, lace and plastic packing material, or organic materials such as tree bark.

Silicone moulds can be useful. I use them alot in Steampunk, and they are great at decorating items such as tea-lights and spoons, or to enhance a model, for example I made a sea bird and used a fish mould to scatter little silver fish around it. There are absolutely loads of silicone moulds available, sometimes sold for cake decorating, which are also perfect for polymer clay.

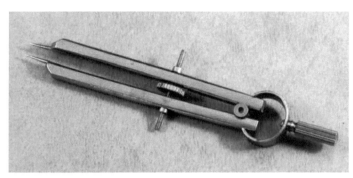

This is a double pointed compass, with two very sharp points which can be adjusted to any width you want. I use this when I want a thin strip of clay a particular width as it's much easier than cutting using a blade. The points will cut through clay rolled on a thin setting, and one of the things I use it for is covering the edge of a pendant.

This is a little tool made for tracing, but it makes wonderful little stitch marks on the patchwork bunny. Unfortunately I didn't buy it until after I'd made about 10 bunnies!

These are Fimo bead piercing needles and come in a pack of 50 needles in two sizes, 0.8mm diamter and 17mm diameter. Both are 90mm long. I use the thinner ones (0.8mm) for piercing beads, and the thicker ones (17mm) for the Christmas Robins and Cat decorations.

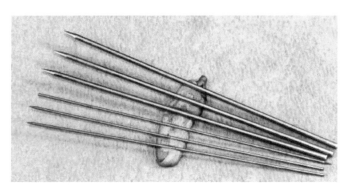

TECHNIQUES USED IN THE BOOK:

Templates:

To make Skinner blends I often use card templates, using a 6cm x 9cm playing card. You could use a similar sized piece of card.

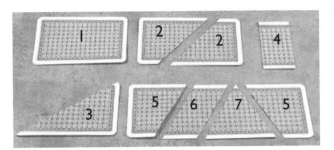

These are the ones I use on a regular basis. I use templates number 2 and 3 in this book, but will show you how I use the others.

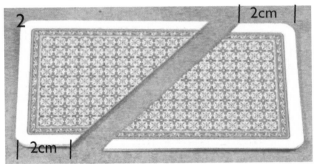

Mark 2cm from the bottom left corner of a playing card, and again from the top right corner. Cut between the lines and you have two templates. I use this template all the time to make Skinner blends.

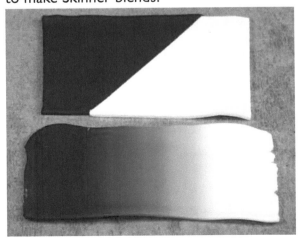

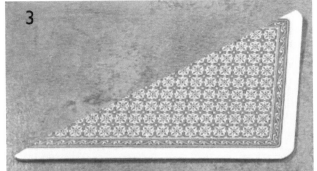

For this template cut the card diagonally from corner to corner. This template makes gradual blends, without any of the two colours (in this case navy and white) showing at the ends. As you can see, neither the navy or the white are pure colours; it's a softer navy as it has a very small amount of white in it, and a very light blue as the white has a very small amount of navy in it.

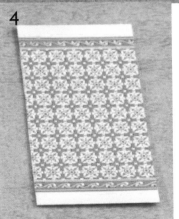

This rectangle measures 6cm x 3cm. It is a perfect rectangle, despite looking slanted in the picture! It is useful when making stacked canes.

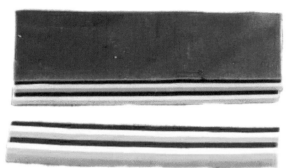

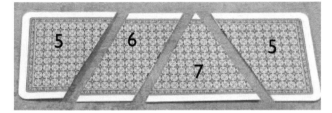

5　6　5

7

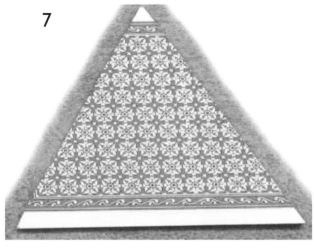

7

7 - this is 6cm high and 6cm along the bottom which makes it the same angle as number 5 template.

This is a really useful shape for adding white into a blend if the two colours either side do not mix, for example purple and green. Purple and green mixed would make a mud colour, but by adding the white triangle, the blend goes from purple to light purple to light green to green.

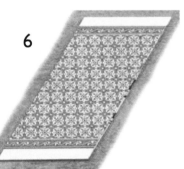

5

5 - This shape has less of an angle than numbers 2 & 3. It is useful when making blends of three colours. It measures 5cm across the top and 2.5cm along the bottom.

6 - this is cut to the same angle as 5, and is 3cm wide. This enables you to add colours in a blend.

6

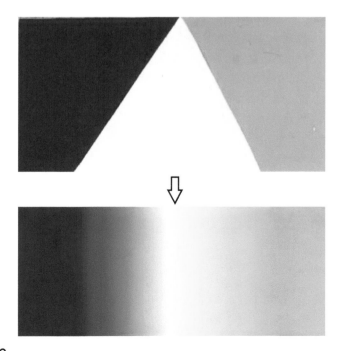

Making a Skinner blend:

Using a standard playing card as a template, or a piece of card 9cm x 6cm, cut out some coloured clay and some white clay.

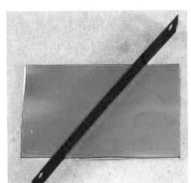

Stack the two clays together and mark 2cm from the bottom left corner and 2cm from the top right corner. Cut between the two marks

Separate the four pieces and put the two dark colours together and the two lighter colours together. Make them into a rectangle as shown above. Roll lightly with your clay roller to help them stick together.

Put the clay through the pasta machine on the thickest setting, dark side one side and white side the other as shown above.

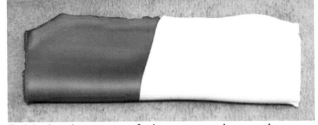

Fold the bottom of the rectangle to the top, keeping the dark colour on one side and the lighter colour on the other.

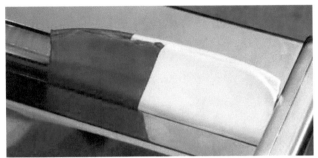

Put through the pasta machine again.

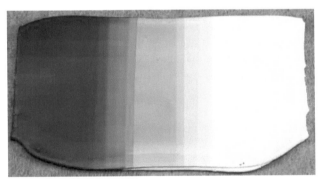

Keep folding the clay and putting it through the pasta machine, making sure that the fold in the clay is put through first and the two colours are on opposite sides. The blend will start to appear as shown above; don't worry that it looks uneven at first, it can take well over 20 times though the pasta machine to get a nice blend.

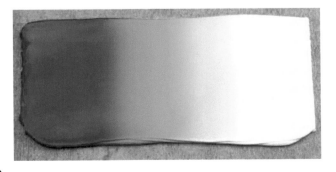

Skinner blend, increasing the darkness on one end:

I adapted this technique from a tutorial from Ivy Niles, an incredibly talented cane maker. She adds some black or other dark colour at one end to increase the depth of colour in the blend, and I've done the same ever since. I got her permission to share it.

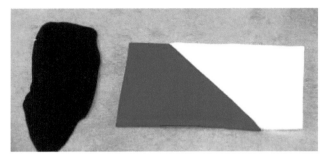

Start off as you would for the Skinner blend shown on the previous page, and roll out some black clay on PM7. I'm using black here but you can use any dark colour that goes with the clay, for example I use dark brown when darkening yellow clay.

Cut a piece of the black clay, the height of the rectangle and 3cm along the bottom edge. Make a curve between the two ends.

Place the thin black clay on the dark clay.

The final blend. I just love this technique, it really makes a difference to my blends, and I'm sure once you've done it once, you'll be adding those thin little black shapes at the end as well!

Mo Clay method of making a blend:

Monica Resta (Mo Clay) uses this method of making small blends which is really easy and quick. She gave permission for me to share it.

Roll logs of the clay you want to make into a blend, I've used two colours, but you can use as many different colours as you like.

Lay the logs side by side and flatten slightly with your clay roller.

Fold the logs over, slightly off-setting them as shown on the third photo on the right.

Put through the pasta machine, short end first,

and continue to fold and put through as you did for the Skinner blend until you have a smooth blend.

Skinner blend to bulls eye cane:

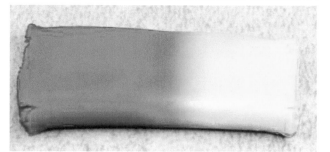

Fold your blend as if you were going to continue making the Skinner blend.

However, this time put it through the pasta machine, short end first, either the light or the dark end, it doesn't matter which. Put through on the thickest setting of the pasta machine, PM0. Then put through again on PM2, PM4 and finally PM6, making a long thin blend.

Decide which end you want to roll up first, which colour you want in the middle of the bulls eye cane, and cut a small piece off, I've cut off around 2.5cm. Roll the cut off piece into a

log and place on the end of the strip.

The rolled up bulls eye cane. Notice there's no little 'hole' in the middle. This is because we made the little log to start off the roll.

Covering a cane with a thin strip of clay:

This is a technique that I do so much as it makes such a difference to canes, in particular bulls eye canes. I often use a strip of clay in white and black, at the thickness of PM6, so that's what I'm using for the demonstration.

Lay your cane on the covering clay, cut a line behind the cane, and two lines the width of the cane, so that the covering clay is the same width as the cane.

Use your clay blade to lift the clay behind the cane to start the rolling, then roll all the way

21

round and a little further. Then roll back a little and you should see a faint line on the covering clay strip. I've made it more obvious on the previous photo by making the line grey to show where it was.

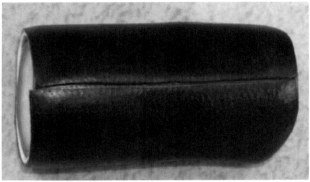

Cut where the line is and you'll find that the two edges will fit nicely together. If there is a little gap just push the two edges gently together.
The photo on the left shows the finished cane.

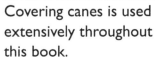
Covering canes is used extensively throughout this book.

How to round the end of a log or a cane:

I round the end of canes or logs a lot in this book, sometimes to hide the scrap clay, and other times to make a nicer, more natural end, for example in the Christmas cat decorations.

First you have a blunt end, in this case I want to hide the dark colour inside.

With your first finger and thumb gently press the outside edges of the top of the log, bringing the top edges inwards.

Continue pressing all the way round, the clay will gradually stretch to cover the end.

Once the end is completely covered, smooth over the end, this can be done by hand, or by rolling on the work surface.

Hollow lentil beads / pendants:

TOOLS & MATERIALS:

- Pasta machine
- Tissue blade
- Craft knife • Ruler
- Oven to cure clay in
- Tile to work on
- Acrylic or metal clay roller
- Needle tool / cocktail stick
- Deli wrap
- Texture sheet, or sandpaper
- Soap stone for burnishing – or a smooth stone, bone folder or credit card can also be used
- Circle cutters 1cm, 12mm and 6cm
- 4.25cm teardrop cutter & 1.5cm heart cutter for chicken
- A variety of small cutters in various shapes, or some Ferrule bootlace crimps – see separate box on right
- Metal bowl to cure pendants on – or any ceramic or metal curved surface
- 80 & 600 grit wet and dry sandpaper
- If you want to varnish the pendant you will need polymer clay varnish. I use Darwi Vernis

Polishing:

- If you prefer to polish your pendant, I use 600 grit wet and dry sandpaper then 1000 grit, then use micro mesh sheets in 1500, 1800, 2400, 3600, 6000 & 12000 for a final finish before polishing with a cloth to a shine.
(All Micro mesh sheets are 6" x 4" and I buy them from ClayAround for £9.59)
I also use Renaissance wax

CLAY:

- 26g (1/2 of a 56g block) each of colour of choice (I used Premo purple), white and black
- Small amounts of other colours for the decoration

Ferrule Bootlace Crimps:

- I use Ferrule bootlace crimps – see the photo above. The ones I use, as shown above are 5mm, 4mm, 3mm, 2mm, 1.5mm & 1mm.
- I use the 5mm and 4mm to make into teardrop shapes, and the 5mm, 4mm and 3mm to make into long petal shapes.

Making the back:

Roll out black clay on PM2, then put through the pasta machine again on PM2 with either a texture sheet, thin sponge, or some sandpaper. You can texture by hand if you prefer.

Cut a 6cm circle and place it on a metal bowl, I use a metal bowl from Ikea. Take a 1cm circle cutter and cut two circles out. These should be 1cm from the edge and in the top half of the black circle of clay. Remove the small circles of clay with your needle tool.

Cure for 1 hour at the clay manufacturers recommended temperature.

Making the Skinner blend:

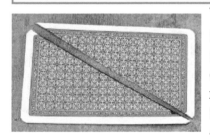

Take a standard playing card, or piece of cardboard 9cm x 6cm and cut in half diagonally as shown.

Roll out the white clay and the coloured clay on PM0, and using one half of the card, cut a piece of each and put together as shown.

Roll some black clay on PM7 and cut a sort of triangular piece with a curved side 6cm tall, and around 2cm wide, shown here, and explained more on page 20.

Place this on the coloured clay, this is going to make the colour darker at the end and make a

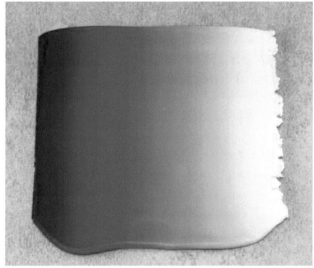

Make a Skinner blend, as shown on page 19.

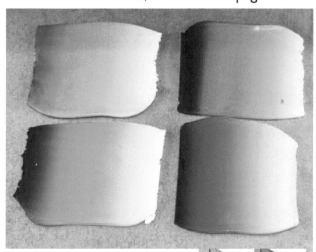

Other coloured blends:
Premo Gold - top left
Premo Fuschia - top right
Premo Peacock Pearl - bottom left
Premo Ultramarine - bottom right

Put the blend through the pasta machine PM1, PM2 then PM3. From now on all the decorations you are going to make will be on PM3. As you are putting the blend through the various settings, be aware that the circle you are cutting is 6cm wide, so you don't want the measurement from light to dark to be much more than that. This way you'll get the full blend in your pendant.

With the 6cm circle cutter, press down just hard enough to make a mark, you don't want to cut all the way through, but it's important to have a mark so your design will fit into the finished pendant. Cut the blend so it is around 1cm

larger than the circle.

Take a piece of deli wrap, cut around 2cm wider than the blend and twice as long. Place the clay on the bottom half, the top half is to fold over and burnish the clay when needed.

Making the Cat:

To make the cat, take the 12mm circle cutter and cut out a circle where you want to bottom of the cat to be.
Roll some black clay to the same thickness (PM3) and cut out a 12mm circle of black clay.

Turn the circle of black clay over and put it in the hole. The reason for turning it is that it makes a better fit.

Fold the deli wrap over the clay and burnish (rub) with the soapstone. This will make the black circle well embedded into the pendant.

Cut another circle, this time 1cm diameter, slightly overlapping the larger circle.

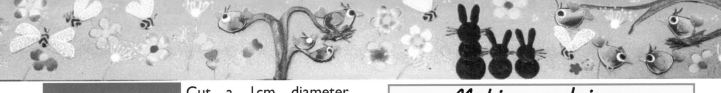

Cut a 1cm diameter circle in black clay, insert and burnish as before. Then cut another 1cm circle, again overlapping the previous circle.
Cut some triangular 'ears' out as shown.

Cut some triangles of black clay, again in PM3, and insert into the ear cuts. Don't worry if they overlap into the circle.

Using the 1cm cutter, re-cut the circle, removing the spare clay from the ears.

Put a circle of black clay in and burnish again. Your cat is nearly complete. You just now need to add the tail.

To make the tail, cut a strip of clay, taking it outside the circle. Replace with an equal size strip of black clay and burnish. Your cat is now complete. Wipe the deli paper with a wet wipe as the black clay will have left a mark.

Making a daisy:

To make a daisy, I first make marks where I want the daisy stem to be with my needle tool. In this pendant I rolled thin logs of green clay. and inserted them, but I prefer to make them by back-filling later. This is explained in the Making Flower Stems section on the next page. To make the daisy petal I've squashed a ferrule bootlace crimp into a longer shape. Cut out a petal, replace with white clay on PM3 and

burnish well.
Continue cutting and filling with petals until you've gone all the way round. For the centre cut a small circle out and replace with yellow clay.

Making a petal flower:

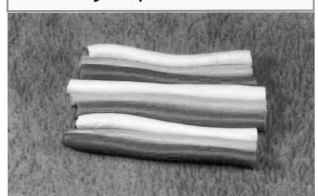

Roll a long thin log of the colour of petal you want, I've chosen pink, another log in a lighter blend of the colour, and another in white. Cut each log into three and lay next to each other.

Lay them dark colour, light colour, white, and repeat. Flatten slightly with your roller, put through the pasta machine on PM0 and fold in half.

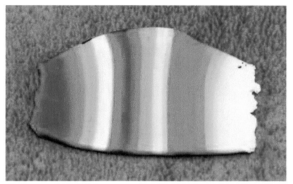

Continue folding and putting through the pasta machine until you have a nice blend of stripes. Finally put the clay through the pasta machine on PM3 with the stripes going downwards.

Once you've completed your design, make sure it's burnished well and put it on the mould. I use metal bowls, but glass ones will be fine too.

Then, with a needle tool or cocktail stick, make fairly deep lines in the clay where you want the flower stems to be, or cat whiskers! Anything in fact that needs a thin line. Now cure your clay for an hour and let it cool.

Using the teardrop shaped cutter, cut five petals from the blend. Cut the first petal shape from the pendant, replace with one of the pieces from the blend, and burnish. Repeat for each of the five petals.

Notice that I haven't put the petals too closely together.

Finally use one of the circle cutters and cut a circle in the middle, and replace with a circle in the colour of your choice.

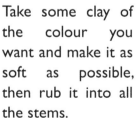

Once cool, keep the pendant on the mould.

Take some clay of the colour you want and make it as soft as possible, then rub it into all the stems.

Wipe off the excess with a baby wipe and put back in the oven for 10 mins to cure. This is also how I do the whiskers.

27

Very basic colour theory:

Making blends for fish:

For the fish I like to make several small blends. Choose four colours, cut a 2cm circle out of each and overlap as shown above. Remembering the colour theory, make sure that no two colours next to each other have three primary colours in them. I like to use whites and neutrals to avoid this.

Roll the overlapped circles with your roller then put through the pasta machine on PM0, fold bottom to top and put through again. Repeat until you have a blend.

Before we make some blends, I just want to explain a little very basic colour theory. Once you have this you'll avoid making blends with 'mud' colour in them.

At the top are the three primary colours: Yellow, Red or Pink, and Blue.

Mix any two of these and you'll get a nice colour, a secondary colour:

Yellow + Pink = Orange
Yellow + Blue = Green
Pink   + Blue = Purple

However, if you add any of a third primary colour, you'll get mud - a browny colour.

So, Purple is made from Pink and Blue, if you add Yellow to it you get mud.

Green has Yellow and Blue in it, so adding Orange, which has Pink in it, makes mud.

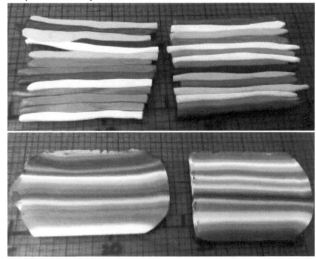

Another way to make a blended stripy sheet is to roll little logs of clay, again thinking of colour theory, and flatten, before making into a blend.

Making the fish:

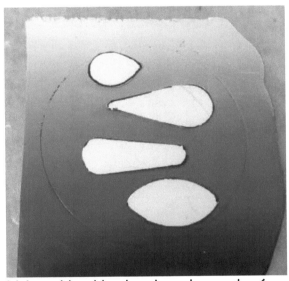

For the fish I use a variety of cutters, as shown above. They have to be small enough to fit on the pendant. However, you don't need these, you can draw fish shapes on cardboard and use them to cut round instead.

Make a blue blend and mark out the 6cm circle. I've cut some card shapes of the cutters and arranged them in the circle. Leave room for the fish tails.

I'm starting with the second fish from the top. Take the cutter and cut from one of the first four blends you made.

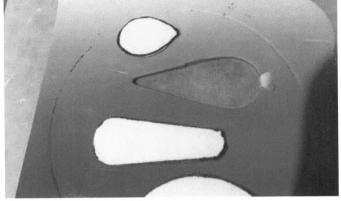

Cut the same shape out of the pendant. You're now going to make the fish mouth and tail before you replace the fish body.

With a 5mm heart cutter, cut a heart shape out from the fatter end of the shape. Cut the same size heart from one of the blends, I've used a yellow and green part of the blend, and put in place. As you can see I've made it so the heart partly overlaps the fish, in which case you use the fish body cutter, or a craft knife, to remove the excess.

To make the tail I used a 5mm teardrop cutter and did the same as for the mouth.

Before replacing the fish body I added the eyes, put a strip of black clay behind the head and put some yellow circle dots in. Once you're happy with it, replace the body and burnish well.

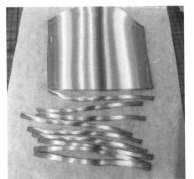

For the second fish I've taken one of the blends and cut around 9 x 2mm strips.

On a piece of deli paper lay the strips side by side, slightly off-setting each one by 2mm. I've made a zig-zag pattern. This is called Bargello.

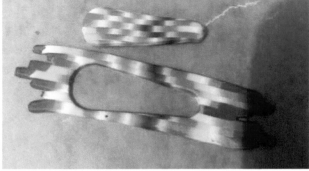

Once the 9 strips are placed, burnish well, then take the fish cutter or cardboard template and cut out the shape, positioning it so you get the colours you want.

For the mouth I've used the 5mm heart cutter, and for the tail I've cut out a triangle of the red part of the bargello.

The completed second fish. Burnish well.

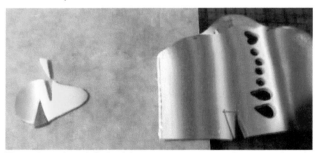

For the third fish (the top one on the pendant), cut out the body shape, then make little triangular shaped cuts in the body and replace with the same shaped triangles cut out of the blended clay.

Continue until you have six triangular inserts. Don't worry that they protrude outside the fish body.

Put in an eye, then re-cut the shape, which will tidy up all the excess clay.

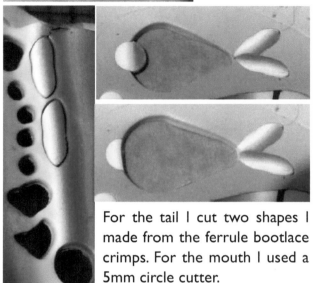

For the tail I cut two shapes I made from the ferrule bootlace crimps. For the mouth I used a 5mm circle cutter.

The completed third fish.

For the final fish cut the body shape then insert strips of blended clay. Burnish then re-cut.

30

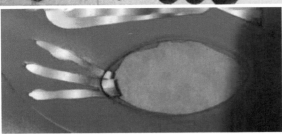

For the tail I cut three strips around 2mm wide, inserted 2mm wide strips of blended clay, then burnished. Finally re-cut the body shape to remove any excess clay from the tail.

Once completed burnish well.

To finish I've put a few fins on the fish, and also added bubbles.

Burnish the whole thing very well before cutting finally with the 6cm cutter and placing on your mould.

Cure for 1 hour. Make sure your oven is pre-heated, you use an oven thermometer, and if possible, cover the clay.

I've spent a long time over a pendant in the past, only to ruin it by not taking sufficient care in the curing.

To make the chicken, make a cardboard template of a 4.25cm teardrop cutter.

Draw in the parts that need to be removed in order to make the chicken's neck and tail feathers (I've coloured them in yellow). Cut out the teardrop shape from the pendant blend, place the cardboard template on the teardrop you've just removed and cut out the yellow parts. Put them carefully to one side.

Next cut a teardrop shape in the colour you want the chicken body to be, and again cut out the yellow parts.

Take the cut out parts from the teardrop you took from the pendant blend and put to one side, and insert them into the gaps in the teardrop in the chicken body colour.

Replace the teardrop in the pendant and burnish well.

This should be done before you add any other decorations such as flowers etc.

For the beak, cut out a triangle and replace with yellow or gold clay. The wattle (bit underneath the beak) is made with a 5mm teardrop cutter, as is the comb (the part on top of the head) which uses three 5mm cut outs. The chicken wing is made using a 1.5cm heart cutter and some of the blend I made for the fish pendant.

Finally, the little spots on the chicken's body were made by making irregular dents and filling with white clay after curing.

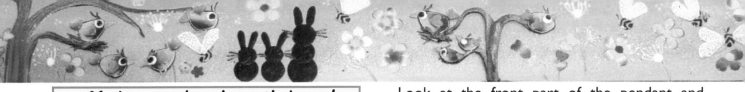

Making the lentil bead pendant:

To make the two pieces of the pendant ready to join you need some wet and dry sandpaper, in 80 or 100 grit.

Wet the sandpaper and place on a flat surface. Take the pendant and wet it, then rub it in a circular motion on the sandpaper. You are looking to create a flat edge all the way round as shown in the photo above. Repeat with the black back part as well.

To complete the process you need some superglue - brush on is easiest to use - and the two pendant parts.

Look at the front part of the pendant and work out where you want the top to be, then make a mark at the back. This is important because you don't want to go to all that effort to make a lovely pendant, then when you hang it the chicken/cat etc is at an angle - you could always say the cat was drunk, but I doubt you'd get away with it!

Brush glue round a third of the pendant, then place the back part on it, making sure that you line up the mark you made on the front piece with the middle of the two holes on the back piece.

Leave it to dry for a few minutes then glue the rest and stick the two parts together.

Once finished you can now either varnish it or polish it. If you use varnish, first sand the front with wet and dry 600 grit then 1000 grit wet and dry sandpaper, then use a polymer clay varnish - I use Darwi Vernis.

Sanding and polishing:

To sand and polish to a high sheen, first use the 600 and 1000 grit wet and dry sandpaper, then the 6 micro mesh cloths, starting with 1500 and working up through the grits until the last one, 12000.

Make sure you rinse the cloth and the pendant between each cloths then polish with a course cloth until it shines. I use renaisance wax on the pendant before I start to polish. A piece of denim is useful to polish with, a dremel with a soft buffing attachment, or for a fantastic sheen, a buffing wheel.

No drama, here comes the Llama:

TOOLS & MATERIALS:

- Pasta machine
- Tissue blade
- Craft knife • Ruler
- Oven to cure clay in
- Tile to work on
- Small tile to cure the llama on approximately 10cm x 10cm
- Acrylic or metal clay roller
- Needle tool / cocktail stick
- Deli wrap. layout paper or just plain white paper
- Soap stone for burnishing – or a smooth stone. bone folder or credit card can also be used
- Polymer clay adhesive – I use Bake and Bond. but any will work
- Circle cutters 8mm. 2cm. 3cm and 4cm – don't buy these especially. you can manage without
- A small cutter around 5mm diameter – this is for the shape in the middle of the bunting so not imperative to the project
- Knitting needles – I use a 3mm diameter one for making the holes for the ears and a 1cm diameter one for blending joins etc
- Toothbrush for texture
- If you want to varnish the pendant you will need polymer clay varnish. I use Darwi Vernis

Tools & Materials continued:
- Tin foill
- 1.2mm wire – I buy mine from garden centres
- Pliers
- Wire cutters

CLAY:

All the clay I've used are 56g blocks of Premo

For the llama body:
- 3 x Pearl
- 1/2 x Bronze
- 1/2 x Black

For the blanket you can use any colours. but if you want to replicate my colours. these are the amounts you'll need.

- 1 x Turquoise
- 1 x Pomegranite
- 1 x Zinc Yellow
- 1 x Copper
- 1 x Fuschia
- 1 x Bronze
- 1 x Bright Green Pearl
- 1 x White
- 1 x Black

Making the Llama coat cane:

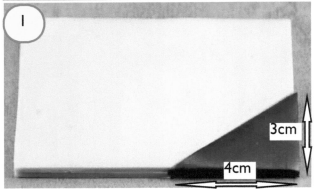

Roll pearl clay on PM0 and cut a rectangle 6cm x 9cm, double thickness (two layers of clay). This is the size of a standard playing card. Cut one of the corners off, the size shown, and replace with two triangles of bronze clay.
Make it into a Skinner blend - for the technique, see page 19.

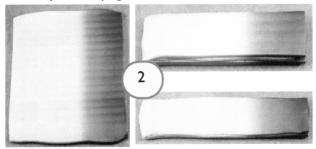

Once you have a smooth blend, cut it into three equal pieces and stack them. Then with your clay roller, roll the stack until it is slim enough to go through the pasta machine. Pinch one of the short ends of the stack.

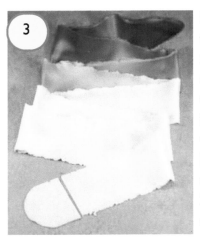

Put it through the pasta machine, pinched end first, on PM0, then PM2, PM4 & finally PM6; you will then have a long blended strip. Cut about 2cm off the pearl end as shown.

Roll the 2cm cut off piece of clay into a log, and place at the end of the strip, then roll up into a bullseye cane.

Roll the cane to 26cm long then flatten it with your roller until it's 30cm.

Cut four of the pieces in half, lengthways as shown.

You're now going to make the cane by putting two pieces together, end to end, this forms the first row. For the second row put one of the half pieces with the cut end to the outside, then a full piece, then another half piece,

again with the cut end outwards.

Repeat these two rows twice more.

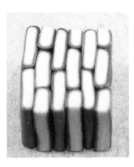

34

Lengthen the cane until it measures about 1cm x 1.5cm diameter.

Making the ears:

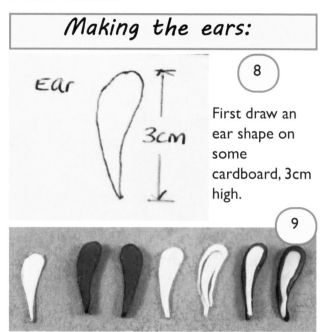

Ear

3cm

⑧

First draw an ear shape on some cardboard, 3cm high.

⑨

Roll some bronze clay on PM2 and cut out two ear pieces. For the inside of the ear cut a strip off the cardboard pattern all the way round, and cut out two pieces in pearl. Place the inside pearl pieces on the bronze one, making sure you have a left and a right ear. Finally, gently pinch all the way round the ears to give the ears a more delicate look.

⑩

To cure, roll up some foil into a log and place the ears on it, curing them over as shown. Cure for 1 hour at the clay manufacturer's recommended temperature.

Making the llama body:

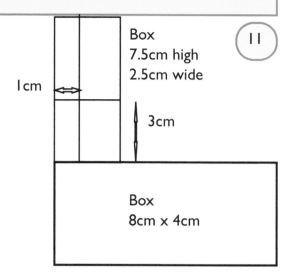

Box
7.5cm high
2.5cm wide

1cm

3cm

Box
8cm x 4cm

⑪

To make the template for the middle of the llama, first cut out in cardboard the shape above. A large rectangle 8cm x 4cm, with another rectangle on the top left of 2.5cm x 7.5cm.
Draw a line horizontally 3cm from the bottom of the top rectangle, and a vertical line 1cm from the left side.

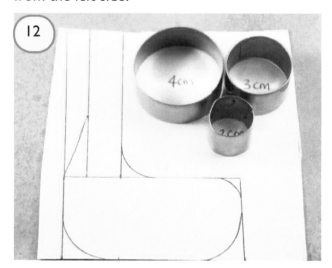

⑫

Draw a line from the bottom left corner of the top rectangle to the point where the two lines crossed. Use three circle cutters to make the curves, 2cm, 3cm and 4cm. The two bottom curves use the 4cm cutter, the top right curve is the 2cm cutter, and the curve between the back and neck uses the 3cm cutter.

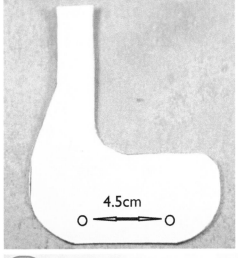

The llama body shape cut out. Make holes as shown with your needle tool.

4.5cm

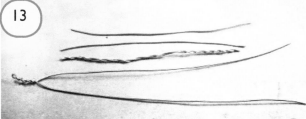

13

Cut your wire as follows:
4 x 16cm   and   1 x 50cm
Twist 2 of the 16cm pieces together, repeat with the remaing two pieces, giving you two 16cm pieces of twisted wire, these will be the legs.
Fold the 50cm piece of wire in half and twist the folded end for 1.5cm (this is the tail).

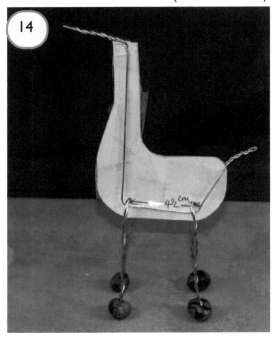

14

Take the two twisted pieces of wire and thread each one through one of the holes in the body. Then take the longer piece of wire and fix (using scotch tape) the folded and twisted end to where you want the tail to be.

Take the longer pieces of wire either side of the body, underneath the two legs both sides, and up the neck to the top. Twist the two pieces of wire that meet at the top of the head, and it should look something like the previous photograph. Secure the wire with scotch tape as you go.

Finally bend the leg wires to make two legs each, so they're 2.5cm apart at the foot end and 1.5cm at the part where they go through the cardboard. They will be this shape:

Body

legs

I put balls of clay on them just so they'd stand up for the photo, you can do this if easier, but it's not necessary.

15

Make three strips of foil, 10cm x 30cm each, and wrap one round the body of the llama.

36

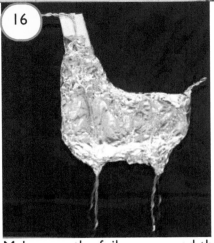

16

Gently press it into the shape of the body, then repeat with the other two strips.

Make sure the foil goes round the top of the legs to secure them in place. Trim the legs so the llama stands up.

Bend the twisted wire at the top of the neck into the position you want the head. I like to make them pointing straight ahead because it gives them their slightly 'snooty' look, but you can having them looking round, up, down, wherever you like best.

17

To give your llama a more rounded body, take some foil, 30cm x 30cm, scrunch it up lightly, then press onto one side of the body. Once on, continue to press it down, shaping it to the shape you want it to be. Repeat the other side, then use a piece of foil 5cm x 30cm to wrap round the body to secure them in place.

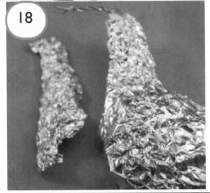

18

Do the same to thicken the neck, and again secure with a long thin strip of foil.

Your llama is now ready to cover with clay.

Making the head:

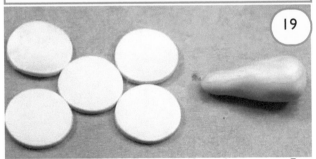

19

Roll some pearl clay on PM0 and cut out 5 x 3cm circles, roll into a ball, then a teardrop shape 4.5cm in length.

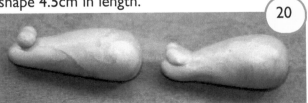

20

For the nostrils roll some pearl clay on PM0 and cut 2 x 8mm circles. roll each into a ball and place them at the narrow end of the teardrop, 1cm from the end. Blend the back of the balls into the head.

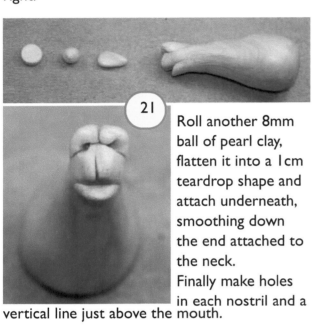

When the balls are well blended into the head, push them down so they're horizontal rather than sticking up, as shown in the picture on the right.

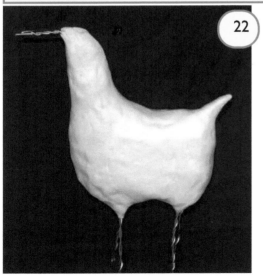

21 Roll another 8mm ball of pearl clay, flatten it into a 1cm teardrop shape and attach underneath, smoothing down the end attached to the neck.
Finally make holes in each nostril and a vertical line just above the mouth.

Covering the body:

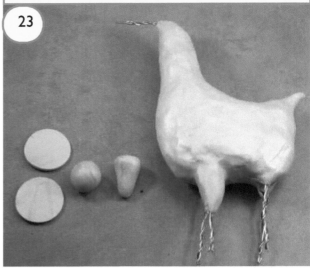

22

Roll pearl clay on PM2 and cover the whole of the llama body. Smooth out any dents by adding little balls of clay and smooth with a large knitting needle.

Making the top of legs:

23

For the top of each leg roll out pearl clay on PM0 and cut out 2 x 3cm circles. Roll them into a ball, then a 2.5cm long cone shape and thread onto the leg. Smooth the clay to join onto the body.

Adding the cane:

24

Take your cane and roll it so it 'squashes' the little brick-like pieces. Make sure you roll the right sides, you what the little bricks to be longer and thinner, not short and fat! Roll it until it's gone down to around 1cm thick.

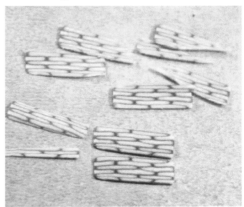

Cut slices as thinly as you can, it doesn't matter if they're aren't whole slices.

38

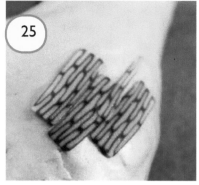

25 Work out where you want the cane pattern to go and start by putting the slices there.

Continue until you've covered all the places you want to.

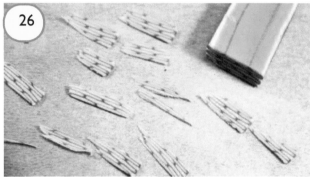

26 You're now going to make very thin slivers of cane that will make the feathered edged on the pattern. Take your blade and don't start cutting at the top of the cane, start a little way down, so you get very thin bits of cane.

27 Add these little slivers of cane round the edges of the pattern; they will look like little hairs, and get rid of the harsh lines of a full cane slice.

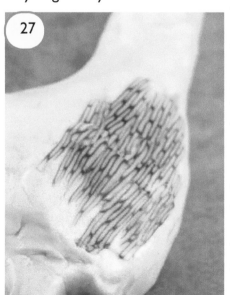

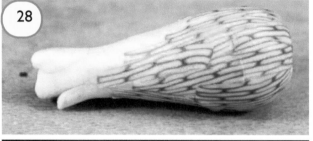

28

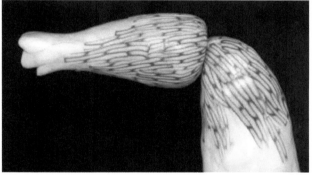

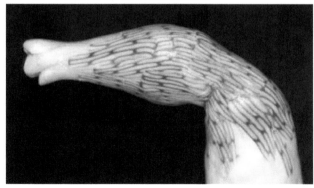

Put the cane pattern you like on the head, then push it onto the twisted wire, being careful not to distort his nose area.
Smooth the join between the head and neck and add more pattern as necessary.

Adding the ears, eyes and mane:

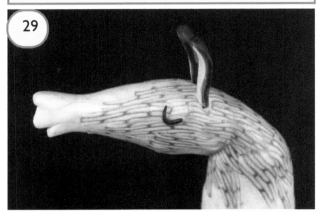

To add the ears, make two holes with a knitting needle approximately 3mm diameter. Put some clay adhesive in each hole and push in the ears, making them lean slightly towards each other and forwards. For the eyes roll some thin logs of clay, tapered at each end, and put on in a U shape as shown.

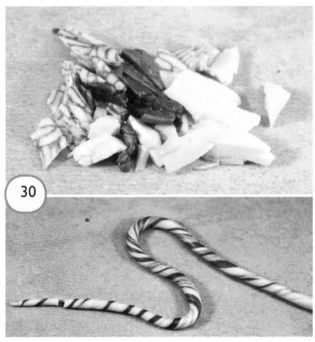

For the mane take some of the scrap clay from the offcuts of the cane, the pearl and bronze. Chop it up then roll into a ball. Roll out into a 2mm log and twist. Taper one end and cut of a 15mm piece. Make around 20 of these little pieces.

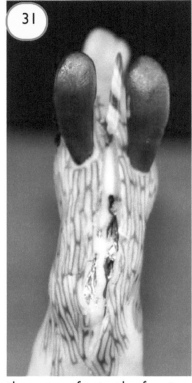

Make a cut in the neck, through the clay to the foil, starting from just in front of the ears, going between the ears, then down to just over half way down the neck.
Put some clay adhesive in the cut.
Starting with one of the tapered mane pieces, push it in the cut, as far to the front as possible.

Continue down the neck, trying to keep the pieces as close as possible. don't worry about arranging them yet.

Once you've got all the way to the bottom, gently close the cut, encasing the mane pieces. Once closed, you can arrange the mane as required.

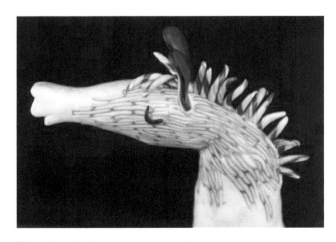

The finished ears, eyes and mane.

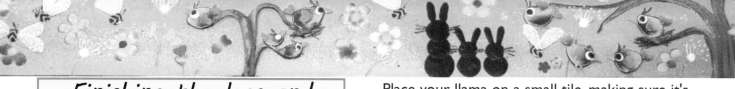

Finishing the legs and feet:

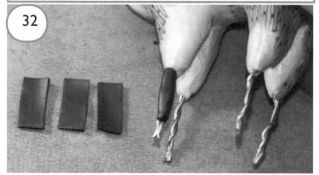

To cover the bottom parts of the legs roll some bronze clay on PM3 and cut 4 pieces of clay 1cm x 2cm. Roll each piece round a leg, leaving the join on the inside.

For the hooves, roll some black clay on PM0 and cut 4 x 3cm circles. Roll them into balls, then cone shape. Push the end of the leg wire into the cone and finish by making an indentation in the front. I use a silicone tool to do this, but you can use anything that will push the clay in rather than cut it.

Curing the llama:

Place your llama on a small tile, making sure it's secure and level. I then like to put it in a box to cure as this keeps it upright when in the oven.

Once in the box, surround your llama with some kitchen paper. Just enough to stop it falling over, not too much or you'll make marks in it. Cure for one hour at the clay manufacturers recommended temperature.

Your llama ready for his (or her) blanket, luggage and decoration (aka the FUN part!)

Mixing the colours:

To make the colours I've used for this llama, mix the clay as follows:
1. 1/2 pack Turquoise (no mixing required!)
2. 1/4 Copper + 1/4 Zinc Yellow
3. 1/4 Pomegranite + 1/4 Zink Yellow
4. 3/8 Bright Green Pearl + 1/8 Pomegranite
5. 1/4 Turquoise + 1/4 Bright Green Pearl
6. 3/8 Zinc Yellow + 1/8 Fucshia
7. 1/4 Copper + 1/8 Pomegranite + 1/8 Bright Green Pearl

These are the colours they made, I wanted a muted palette that was similar to the colours of some of the Peruvian blankets I looked at.

And these were the remaining amounts of colour, plus the 1 packet of black and white.

Cane 1:

There are a lot of stripes in Peruvian blankets!

Roll out some white clay and a colour of your choice (I've used number 7) on PM0 and cut out the above shape, which is 6cm x 9cm, with the diagonal line 2cm from each corner.

For the black piece, roll some black clay on PM7 and cut the clay in the shape shown, then fold it and put through the pasta machine several times to make a darker Skinner blend, as shown on page 19 and 20.

Cut the blend in half and stack the two pieces. Pinch one of the short ends, I've pinched the darker end, before putting through the pasta machine, short dark end first, on PM0, then PM2, PM4 and finally PM6. You will then have a long thin blended piece of clay.

Fold the clay, backwards and forwards, in a concertina or fan fold, making it 2.5cm wide. It doesn't matter whether you start with the white end or the dark pink end, you will end up with a plug of graduated colour.

Roll the plug lengthways until it measures 4cm, then put it through the pasta machine on PM0, short end first. You'll then have a thin strip with white on one side and dark pink on the other.

Roll some black and white clay on PM0 and cut a 5cm piece of each, the width of the pink and white strip you've just made. Stack the black and white clay and pinch one of the short ends. Put through the pasta machine on PM0, PM2 and PM4.

Lay the pink piece, dark side down, on the black side of the thin black/white strip, and trim to shape. Cut in half where shown --------

Roll some green clay (mix number 5) on PM2 and cover the black/white side (not the side showing in the photo above) of ONE half only. Stack the other half on top, black/white side next to the green, and roll until it is 7mm thick.

The cane is stacked as follows:
White - dark pink blend
Thin black/white blend, black next to the pink
Green layer
Thin black/white blend, white next to green
Dark pink - white blend

The finished cane.

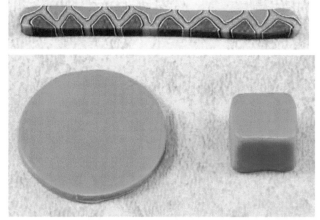

Start by rolling some orange clay, number 6 of my blends, on PM0 and cut a 4cm circle. Roll into a ball and then a cube.

Roll some black and white clay on PM0 and cut a rectangle of each, 8cm - 2.5cm.
Lay one on top of the other, pinch one short end, and put through the pasta machine, short end first, on PM0, PM2 & PM4.

Trim one short end, lay the cube on the white side, and cut the width of the strip to the same width as the cube. Roll the strip round the cube and cut where it meets.
Roll out some ocre clay, number 2 of my colours, on PM2, and cover the cube.
Now make another cube using a different colour inside (I've used brown, number 4), and the same black/white strip and ocre.

43

Cut both cubes in half diagonally.

Cut one of the halves in half again, I've cut the lighter coloured one, and put together as shown.

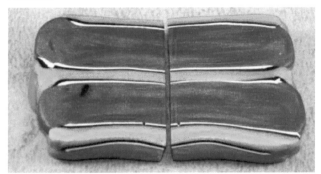

Leave the clay to rest for an hour, then lengthen to 5cm long. Cut in the middle.

Place the two pieces side by side, reduce until it measures around 2.5cm x 0.5cm on the pattern end.
When you make the blanket you'll cut two slices and put them together.

Cane 3:

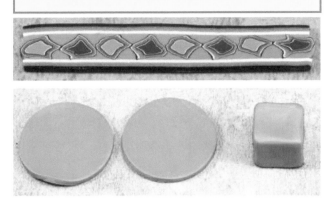

Roll some turquoise clay on PM0 and cut 2 x 4cm circles - roll these into a ball then a cube. Repeat to make a second cube, these are going to form the background colour.

Roll some bronze clay on PM0 and cut a 4cm circle - roll into a ball then a cube. Cover the cube with some of the black/white strip you made for cane 2, then another colour (I've used number 2) on PM0. Finally cover again with the black/white strip (as shown below).

Make another cube, same dimensions as the first one, but in different colours. I've used numbers 5 and 6.

Cut one of the turquoise cubes into four diamond shapes, and place round one of the coloured cubes as shown. Repeat with the second turquoise and coloured cube.

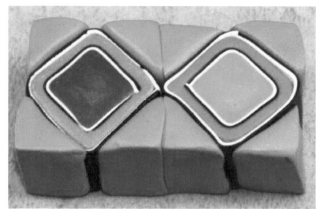

Put the two cubes together as shown.

Reduce the cane to around 14cm long and 1.5cm wide, cut off the distorted ends and cut into four. Lay the four pieces side by side. Roll to the thickness of 5mm.

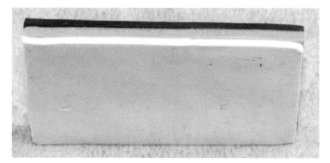

Roll white clay on PM4 and cut a piece the size of the cane. Add ocre on PM2 then black on PM4. Roll with your roller to adhere the three layers.

Put through the pasta machine on PM0 and PM2, so it becomes twice the size of the cane.

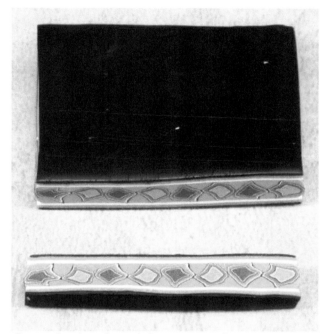

Cover both sides of the cane and cut to size.

Cane 4:

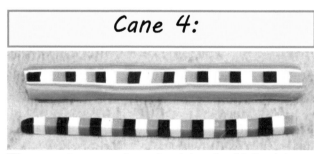

These stripes can be edged (top) of left plain.

Roll ocre, white and black clay on PM2 and cut 4 squares, 2cm x 2cm of each. I cut the ocre square first, lay it on the white and cut round, then the black.

Stack the four ocre/white/black pieces, then cut in half as shown.

Lay the two half pieces side by side, making a longer stack.

Cut the piece into three slices.

Put each slice through the pasta machine on PM0, with the stripes vertical.
You can either leave it as it is, or you can cover both sides, in the same way you did for cane 3.

I used white, orange and green (number 5) to cover the stripes.

This is a flower cane I used to make the material for the parcel on top of the blanket.

Roll white and no 7 colour on PM0, make a Skinner blend as you did in cane 1.

Cut the cane into two; one piece a 1/4 of the blend, and the other 3/4.

Take the larger piece and fold in half as if you were going to continue making a blend. Pinch one of the short ends and put it through the pasta machine, short pinched end first, on PM0, PM2, PM4 & PM6, making a long thin blend.
Fold in a fan fold, 1.5cm folds, white end first, then when almost at the end, fold the dark end of clay around the whole plug.

Put the smaller piece through the pasta machine on PM2, PM4 & PM6, short end first, then cut around 3cm off the white end.

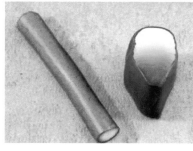 Roll the 3cm piece of clay into a log, lay it on the white end and roll up. Pinch the larger plug into a petal shape.

You now have the two canes ready to make the flower petal

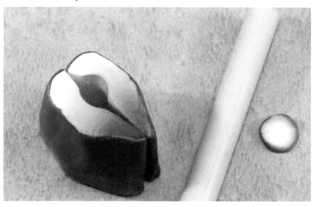

Roll the smaller cane to 8cm and cut in half. Roll one half to 4mm diameter. Take a 5mm circle cutter and make a mark near the top of the larger cane. Cut the petal cane in half as shown above, and using the 5mm circle cutter, cut the two halves of the circle.

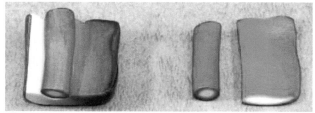

Cut a piece of the 4mm diameter cane to fit into the hole you made. Take another piece of the 4mm cane, cut it the same length and

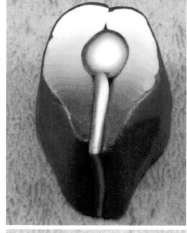

Put the two halves of cane back together, with the 4mm diameter cane and the flattened piece of cane in as shown.

Reduce the cane to 12cm long, cut off the distorted ends and roll again to 12cm.

Cut 6 x 2cm pieces. Cut a 2cm piece of the bullseye cane and arranged as shown on the left.

Roll the colour you want to use as the background, I've used turquoise, into a log 12cm x 5mm diameter. Cut it into 6 x 2cm pieces and pinch one long side of each piece, making them into a triangular shape. Insert these in between the six petals.

Roll the background colour on PM3 and cut rectaangles 2cm long by the measurement of the triangular piece outside edge.

With your thumb and first finger, pinch the two long edges of each of the six flat pieces, and put in between the petals.

Lengthen the cane to around 7mm diameter and cut thin slices. Lay the slices on a piece of the background colour and burnish well.

Strip using bullseye cane:

Take the remaining half of the bullseye cane from the petal cane and roll to 7mm diameter.

Roll some clay you want as the background on PM3, cut thin slices of the bullseye cane, place on the strip and burnish well. Make a strip 6cm long.

Making the blanket:

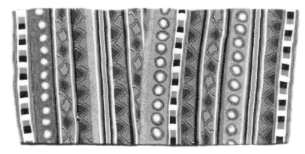

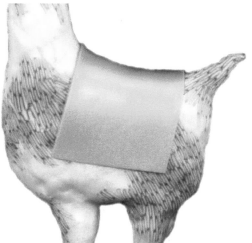

Roll some copper clay on PM3 and cut a rectangle to the size and shape you want it. As the neck end is higher than the back end, if you want the blanket edge to be horizontal you'll need to make it longer on the front edge. If you look at the blanket above you'll see that I've done this. Don't worry about the pattern not matching in the middle, this will be covered by a package.

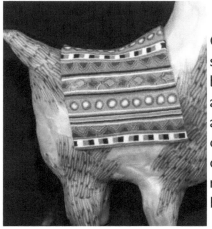

Cut thin strips of the blanket canes, approx 1mm, and lay them on the copper rectangle. Burnish well.

48

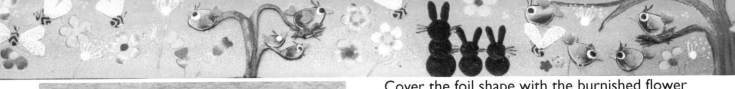

Use a toothbrush to texture the blanket to make it more realistic. The blanket piece on the left is untextured. Put the blanket to one side.

Take a piece of foil 15cm x 30cm and loosely roll it into a ball. Then press it onto the llama back, moulding it into a parcel shape.

Take some turquoise, or whichever colour you used as the background for your flower cane, and roll it on PM3. Cut very thin slices of the flower cane and place on the background colour. Burnish well.

 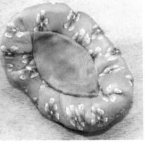

Cover the foil shape with the burnished flower cane 'material', and put a piece of scrap clay in the middle underneath to cover the whole of the underside of the parcel. Push it again onto the llama back to make sure the shape fits.

Take some bronze clay and roll it to two thin logs, around 2mm diameter, then twist them again to make some rope.

Make enough rope to wrap round the parcel, and a little extra for the end of the rope. The overlap in the blanket will be covered

Press again onto the llama's back to make sure it's still the right shape, and put aside.

Put some polymer clay adhesive all over the underside of the blanket and lay on the llama.

Roll some clay on PM2, cut a strip the width of the blanket and around 5mm high, put clay adhesive on it and stick it on the llama at the bottom of each blanket edge. With a craft knife make little fringe cuts, easing them apart a little.

Finally place the parcel on top of the blanket and push down well. Cure the llama for 1 hour, in the box as before.

49

For the top package take some foil 15cm x 15cm and roll it into a small rectangular package around 4cm x 2cm. Put it on the flower parcel and push down so it's the right shape to fit.

Roll some scrap clay to a size that will cover the package, then take 3mm logs of clay in various colours and lay them side by side as shown.

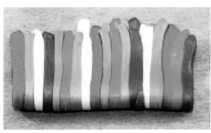

Roll the logs with your clay roller to adhere then fold and put through the pasta machine on PM0. Continue folding and putting through on PM0 until you have a nice blend.

Put the blend on the scrap clay and put through the pasta machine on PM0, PM1 & PM3. Cover the package and push on the flower parcel to again make sure it's fitting well.

Roll some copper clay on PM4, cut 4mm strips and place round the parcel.

With a small ball tool or needle tool make 'stitch marks' along the strip. Put this to one side while you add the bunting and final decorations.

For the bunting string, you can use just a plain strip of clay, but I like to use more colours. Roll white clay on PM2, number 2 colour and bronze on PM0, and black on PM4. Cut a rectangle 1cm x 4cm, roll with your clay roller then pinch the two short ends. Put through the pasta machine on PM0, fold with the white inside and put through again on PM0 and PM2.

Cut thin slices to make the bunting string.

Put some polymer clay adhesive on one side of a strip of bunting string and place round the llama's neck. You will have to join a few together.

An easy way to cut the bunting flags is to roll some clay on PM2 and cut a rectangle 1.5cm x 4cm. Next make marks every 2cm along one long side. Along the other long side make a mark at 1cm, then 3 at 2cm, leaving 1cm gap. Cut between the lines as shown above, making 7 triangles. You could of course just make a triangle pattern and cut round it, the flags are 1.5cm x 1cm.

I like to add some detail to the bunting so using 3/16" cutters in a heart or circle shape, cut a hole and replace with another colour. Burnish well.

Make around 20 bunting flags. these are the ones I made.

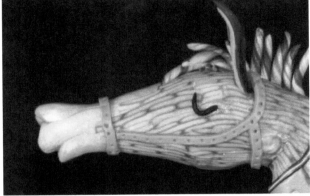

For the simple headcollar, roll some turquoise cay on PM3 and cut 3mm strips. Cover the underside of the strip with polymer clay adhesive and place on the on the llama's head. Finally put little holes along the straps, this is optional, using either a small ball tool or your needle tool.

Put polymer clay adhesive on the side of the bunting flags you want to go on the llama and place along the string, alternating colours.

To finish, put polymer clay adhesive on the underside of the top package and place on the flower parcel, pushing down gently to adhere. Place the llama back in the box you've been curing her, and cure for 1 hour.

If you like to varnish her, you can varnish her with any polymer clay varnish, either in gloss or satin/matt, but I use Darwi Vernis gloss.

Patchwork Bunny and Chicken:

TOOLS & MATERIALS:

- Pasta machine
- Flexible tissue blade
- Craft knife
- Ruler
- Oven to cure clay in
- Tile to work on
- Acrylic or metal clay roller
- Needle tool / cocktail stick
- Deli wrap
- Soap stone for burnishing – or a smooth stone. bone folder or credit card can also be used
- large knitting needle
- Sponge. sandpaper or other texture for ear
- Alumimium tin foil
- Circle cutter 3cm and also a 5mm one if you have it
- 600 grit wet and dry sandpape
- 1mm ball tool
- 1mm wire – I buy this from a garden centre. it's not seen so doesn't have to be nice wire
- If you want to varnish the pendant you will need polymer clay varnish. I use Darwi Vernis
- Thin wire for the whiskers
- 2 x 4mm black glass beads for eyes. you need two per animal
- 2mm drill bit for the bunn
- If you have a stitch marker. this makes making the stitches much easier than using a ball tool or needle tool

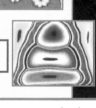

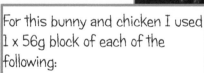
CLAY:

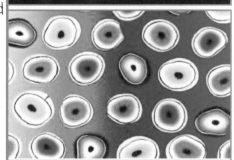

For this bunny and chicken I used 1 x 56g block of each of the following:

- Premo Peacock Pearl
- Premo Wasabi
- Premo Ultramarine
- Premo Fuschia
- Premo Pearl
- Premo Zinc Yellow

And:
- Around half a large (545g) block of Premo White
- 1 x 56g block of Premo Black
- Approximately 2 x 56g blocks of scrap clay

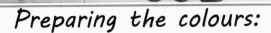

Preparing the colours:

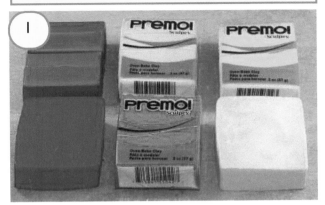

These are the 6 x 56g blocks of Premo clay I've used to make the colours. If you'd like to use your own, you will need 10 x 1/2 blocks of colour.

1 = 1/2 a block of Premo Peacock pearl
2 = 1/4 block of Premo Peacock pearl
    1/4 block of Premo Wasabi
3 = 3/8 block of Premo Ultramarine
    1/8 block of Premo Pearl
4 = 1/2 block of Premo Wasabi
5 = 1/2 block of Premo Fuschia
6 = 3/8 block of Premo Pearl
    1/8 block of Premo Ultramarine
7 = 1/2 block of Premo Zinc yellow
8 = 1/4 block of Premo Zinc yellow
    1/4 block of Pearl
9 = 1/4 block of Premo Fuschia
    1/4 block of Premo Ultramarine
10 = 1/4 block of Premo Zinc yellow
    1/4 block of Premo Fuschia

Put the reamaining four peices of Pearl, Peacock pearl, Wasabi and Ultramarine to one side to be used later.

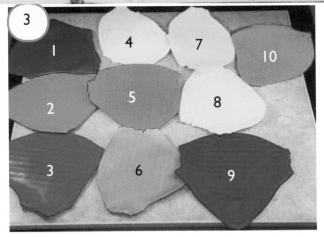

Mix the colours. If any of the colours (or the white and black) are too soft or sticky, leach them by rolling on PM0 and putting between 2 sheets of white paper, with a weight on top. After around an hour you'll see that oil will have leached out, making the clay stiffer.

Cane 1 - spots:

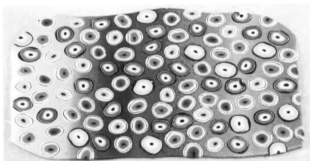

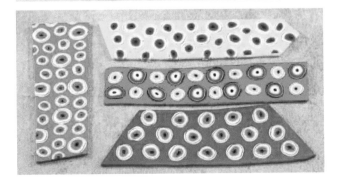

4 Roll one of the colours and white clay on PM0. Cut 2 x 3cm circles of each.

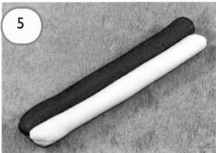

5 Roll the white and colour into logs, 8cm long. Place side by side and flatten a little with your roller.

6 Fold, off-setting at the end as shown in the picture.

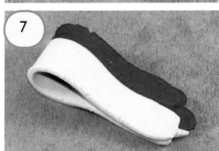

7 Put through the pasta machine on the thickest setting, fold over and repeat until you have a smooth blend.

8 Fold the blend in half and roll gently.

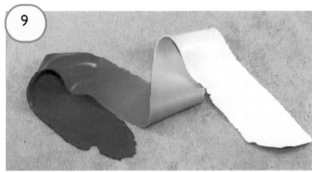

9 Put the clay blend through the pasta machine on the thickest setting (PM0), lengthways this time ie with either the white end or coloured end first. Repeat on PM2, PM4 and finally PM6 until you have a long thin blend.

10 Roll some black clay to 3mm diameter log and place along the bottom of either the dark or white end. I've chosen the dark end for this cane.

Roll up firmly into a bullseye cane.

If you don't want a spot in the cane, leave out the little roll of black clay.

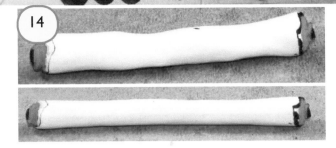

Roll some white clay and black clay on PM0. Cut a rectangle the width of the cane and 12cm long. Put them together and pinch one end. This is so that the two clays don't separate when you put them through the pasta machine.

Run through the pasta machine, short pinched end first, on PM0, then PM2, PM4 and PM6.

Continue squeezing and gently pulling to bond the layers and lengthen the cane. When it reaches 8cm, you can roll it to make it smooth. Cut off the distorted ends and cut the cane in half.

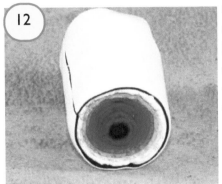

Cover the cane with the black/white strip, putting the black on the inside.

If the outside of the cane is the darker colour as in this cane, you'd cover it with the white side of the black/white strip on the inside.

Continue with as many colours as you like, I've made 7, some with the dark colour on the inside, some with the white. It's totally up to you whether you put the black log in the middle, if you'd prefer the canes without the inside dot, leave it out.

Cane 1 - vaneer:

These templates are made from clay.

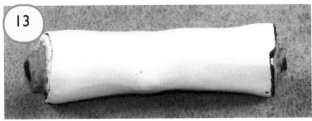

Once you've made the cane, you need to really make sure that all the layers are bonded, so squeeze the cane all the way along. Don't worry that it will look 'mangled', it will be fine, but it's important you don't have any air bubbles in it.

I use these templates to make the blended background for one of the spot vaneers. The triangle measures 4cm across the bottom and is 5cm high. The shape on the right is exactly half the size of the larger triangle.

I learnt about these triangles from Marie Segal when I was lucky enough to attend a workshop with her a few years ago.

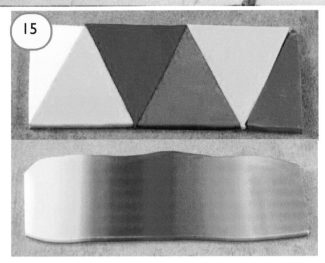

Roll the white, yellow pearl (4), dark blue (3), pink/yellow mix (10) and light blue clay (6) on PM0, and cut triangles as shown above.

Put through the pasta machine on PM0 until you have a nice blend. Once blended, put through the pasta machine on PM3; it is now ready to add the spots.

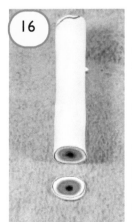

Roll the canes to the diameter of spots that you want and cut thin slices. You can have spots of different sizes or all the same size, it is totally up to you. Try and cut the slices as thin as possible as this will reduce the risk of them distorting too much.

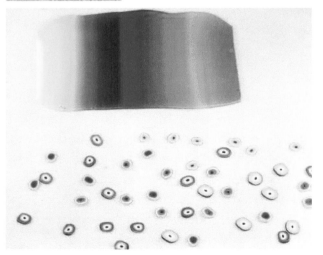

Put the blended clay on a folded piece of deli wrap. Add the spots.

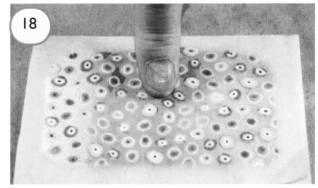

Fold the top of the deli wrap over, and first push down every spot with your thumb or finger; this pushes each spot down into the blend so that when you burnish it, the spots are less likely to spread.

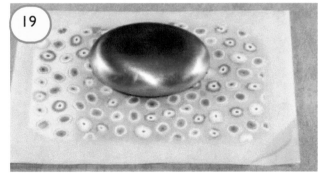

Finally burnish the vaneer. Burnishing is rubbing the clay so that all the parts (spots and blends in this case) are smooth, without any ridges, lumps or bumps. I use a soap stone, but you can use an old credit card, a bone folder, the back of a spoon, a smooth pebble, or anything that you can rub over the deli wrap and smooth out the clay.

Cane 2 - Celtic knot:

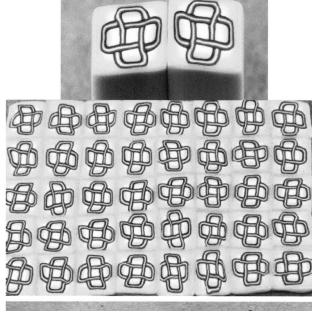

2cm

2cm

I

For the blends in this cane I use the template above. It's a standard playing card, measuring 9cm x 6cm, cut diagonally 2cm from the bottom left corner and top right corner.
Roll white and yellow clay out on PM0 and cut to the shape of the template. I've used yellow and white but you can use whichever colour and white you prefer.

2

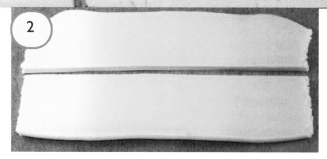

Put through the pasta machine on PM0, make into a Skinner blend, following instructions on page *.
Once in a blend, cut it in half as shown above.

3

Stack one piece on top of the other and pinch one of the short ends, I've pinched the white end. This is so that when you put it through the pasta machine the two pieces don't split apart.

4

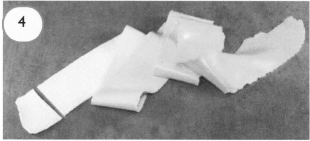

Put the stacked clay through the pasta machine on PM0, the pinched end first, then put through again on PM2, PM4 and finally PM6 until you have a long thin strip. Cut around 2cm off the white end.

5

Roll the piece of white clay you cut off into a log and place at the end of the long strip.

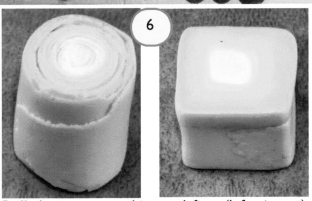

Roll the strip up, white end first (left picture). Now make this into a cube, 2cm high (right picture). Put this to one side while you make the second blend.

Roll one of the darker colours and white on PM2 and cut the same shaped template as you did for the first blend. Roll some black clay on the thinnest setting you can and make a curved triangle shape as shown above. This will make a far more intense blend. Make it into a Skinner blend.

Cut it in half, stack and pinch one short end.

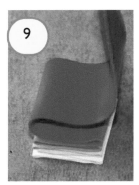

Put through the pasta machine on PM0, PM2, PM4 & PM6, then you're going to fold it up in a fan fold, making each fold 2cm wide. You will end up with a graduated blended block, I call a plug.

Roll some black clay on PM3 and cover the darker side of the plug.

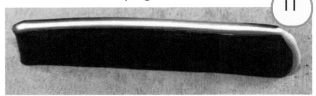

Using your roller, lengthen the block, keeping it around 2cm wide, and alternating between rolling the dark side and the white side, until it is thin enough to put through the pasta machine on PM0. Trim the long edges so it measures 2cm wide.

Cut the strip into four equal size pieces. They will be around 4cm long each, but you can get away with as little as 3cm if by some chance your strip is shorter than 15-16cm.

Return to the yellow cube and cut 4mm off all four sides. Cut two opposite sides first, put the off-cuts to one side then cut the other two, shorter sides.

Taking the square left, mark it into 9, then cut.

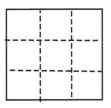

58

You're going to use the centre square for the next stage.

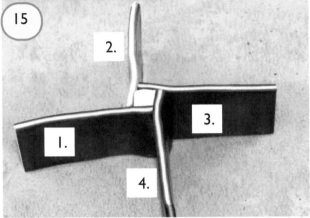

15

2.

3.

1.

4.

Take one of the flat strips and place on one side of the white centre part, in line with one edge. Take the second flat strip and place it on another of the white sides, up against the first strip. Repeat with the third and fourth strips.

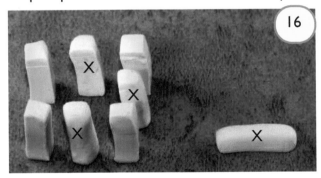

16

X

X

X

X

Take the four middle pieces (marked by X) and round the outside edge. Do this by putting the piece flat down on the work surface, inside edge downwards.
With your first finger and thumb in each hand, gently pinch the top of the piece so it becomes rounded. Place each piece in the cane as shown.

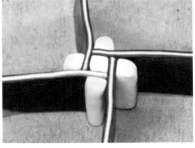

17

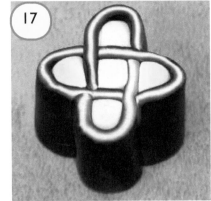

Fold each flat piece round, cutting to size so they fit neatly against the next flat piece.

18

Take each of the four remaining corner pieces. As shown in the picture, have the inside lighter-coloured corner facing you, then gently pinch the two corners either side so the piece becomes wider and more of a diamond shape.

19

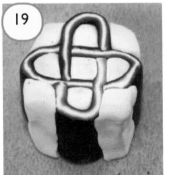

Place the four corner pieces back in the cane.

Finally replace the four pieces that you cut off earlier.

20

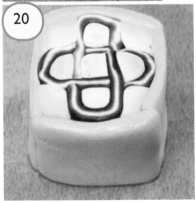

Don't worry that the four pieces don't fit; just stretch them so they cover each side.

Cane 2 - vaneer:

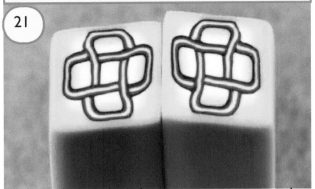

Reduce the cane to the size you want to make the vaneer out of.

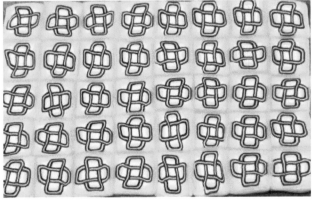

Roll some scrap clay on PM5, cut thin slices of cane and place, butted up against each other, on the sheet. As you did with the cane 1 vaneer, place between two sheets of deli paper and burnish well.

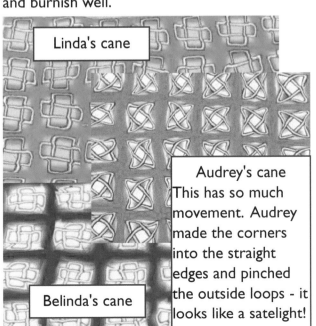

Linda's cane

Audrey's cane
This has so much movement. Audrey made the corners into the straight edges and pinched the outside loops - it looks like a satelight!

Belinda's cane

Cane 3 - Right angles:

Take the 1/4 block of ultramarine, roll out on PM0 and cut 12 x 2cm circles. Take some white clay, also rolled on PM0, and cut out 16 x 2cm circles.
These will make the four blends of blue.

1 = 6 x ultramarine, 1 x white
2 = 3.5 x ultramarine, 3.5 x white
3 = 2 x ultramarine, 5 x white
4 = 0.5 x ultramarine, 6.5 x white

Thoroughly blend the four colours with the pasta machine and you will end up with the blends above. Roll them all on PM0.

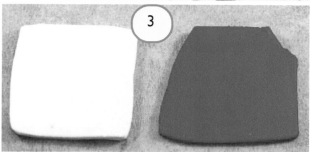

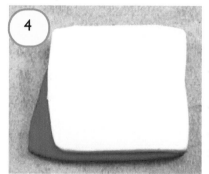

You need to make each of the four colours into a square shape. This is the way that I do this. The light blue on the left is in a square shape, but you can see the darker one is far from square.

Put the square shaped clay on top of the mishapen one. Trim the blue clay that's sticking out.

Roll some white clay on PM0, place the squares on it, and cut round. Do this with all four.

On the dark square only (far right), cover both sides with white.

Put the bits of blue that you cut off onto the blue clay to make a square.

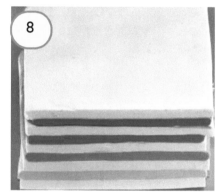

Stack the four squares as shown.

Cut the stack into four smaller squares.

Finally, put the blue clay through the pasta machine a few times to make it smooth.

Put each square on its side, and making sure the stripes are on the top, cut diagonally through, making two triangles.

61

Make four squares as shown. You will need to take one half from one square and put it with another half from another square in order to

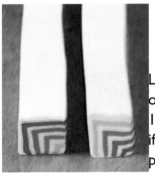

match up the colours, making two different types of cane.

Lengthen one of each of the canes to around 1cm square, or smaller if you want a smaller pattern.

Cane 3 - vaneer:

Cut thin slices of the cane, turning it a quarter turn after each cut, which will help to keep the slices square.

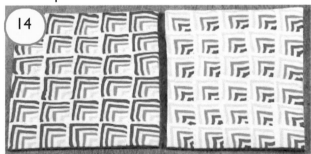

Roll some offcuts of the blue and white clay on PM5, place the slices of clay on it and burnish as you did for the first two vaneers.

You can also alternate the two cane slices to make a slightly different vaneer.

Cane 4 - Daisy:

Roll white clay on PM0 and cut a 6cm x 9cm rectangle (standard playing card size). Cut a corner off the white and replace with yellow.

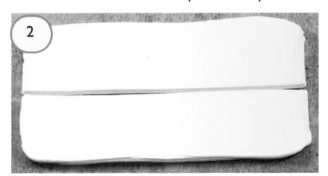

Make into a Skinner blend, then cut in half as shown.

Stack the two halves and pinch one end, I've pinched the white end. Then put through the pasta machine on PM0, PM2, PM4 & PM6.

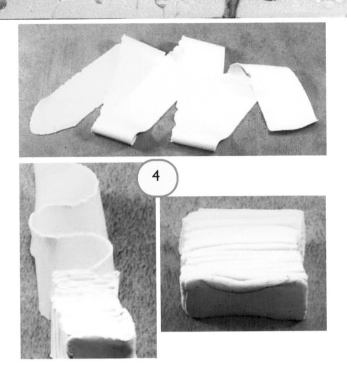

Lay the log on the black/white clay, black side uppermost, with the yellow end of the log facing you. Cut a straight line behind the log and roll the log along the strip to cover.

Fold the long strip of clay in a fan fold, as you did for the purple clay in the celtic knot cane.

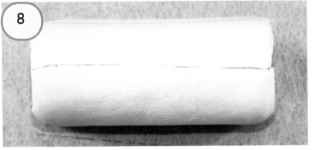

The join line is a good way of knowing where the middle of the white end of the cane is.

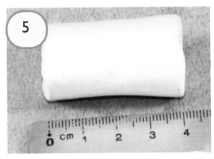

Gently roll the edges of the block until you make a cylinder shape. Roll to 4cm long.

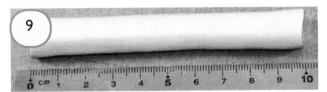

Lengthen the cane to 10cm, cut off any distorted ends and roll again to 10cm.

Roll some black clay on PM4, the width of the log (4cm) and around the same height. Roll some white clay, also on PM4 and stack them. Put through the pasta machine on PM3, then PM4, PM6 & PM8. You will have a very thin piece of black/white clay.

Gently press along one edge of the cane, where the join is so you make a petal shape.

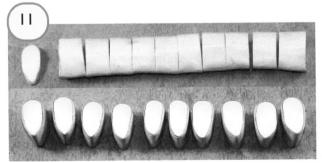

Cut the cane into 10 x 1cm wide pieces. Make sure they're all 'petal-shaped'.

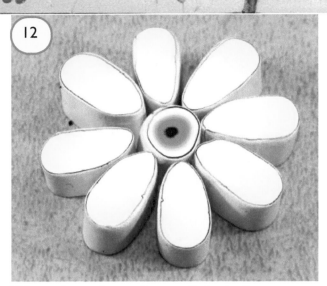

12

Take a 1cm piece of one of the bullseye canes you made earlier, and arrange the petals round it. I've only used 8 petals, but if you had a larger middle you'd probably need all 10.

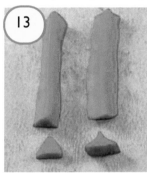

13

Decide what colour you want the outside of your daisy to be and roll a 10cm piece. Make it into a triangle (left), then pinch the top between thumb and finger and push down, making the shape on the right.

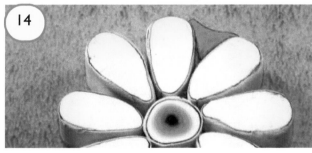

14

Cut 1cm pieces off and insert between the petals.

15

Roll some more of the outside clay and cut a strip, around the size of the middle of one petal to the middle of another. Pinch along the two long sides.

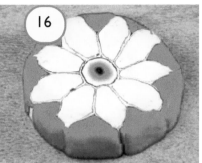

16

Put the pieces in between the petals. If you didn't do this it is likely that your petals would have flat ends.

Finally, roll some more clay out on PM4 and wrap round. You're now ready to reduce the cane.

Keeping the cane flat on the work surface, start to press all the way round. Turn it over and press again.

This is the side view. Keep pressing and gently pulling until it lengthens. Being such a small cane, and only 1cm high

17

it is not easy to reduce, but is possible with a bit of care. A larger cane would be easier, but not needed for this project.

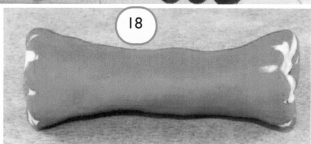

Once long enough, squeeze from the middle, making sure as much as possible that you keep then ends from distorting too much. Press from the middle towards each end. There are various ways to lengthen and reduce a cane, this is my favourite but if you prefer a different method, go for it!

Lengthen to 12cm, then cut off the distorted ends.

Roll again to 12cm and cut in half. I always cut canes in half and only reduce one half, then if I roll it too small, I've still got the other half. Put one 6cm piece to one side and reduce the other to around 6mm diameter.

Cane 4 - vaneer:

Cut thin slices and place on a sheet of the same clay as you put round the daisy. Cover with deli wrap and burnish.

Cane 5 - Helix:

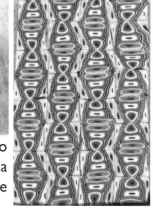

I couldn't think what to call this cane, it looks a little like DNA, hence the name.

This is a cane which uses some of the spare pieces of bullseye cane you've already made. Take 5 pieces, 4cm long, 1cm diameter. If you want the lines (in my vaneer they're yellow) to be one colour, make sure you have two canes of either the same, or very similar colours. I've used the two yellow canes for mine.

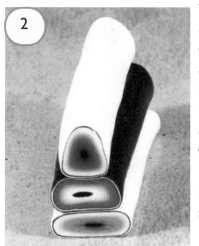

Take the three canes you want the middle part of the pattern to be.

Flatten the first one to 1.5cm wide (pink)

Flatten the second one to 1cm wide (blue)

and the top one to around 8mm wide and pinched at the top in a triangular shape (purple).

65

3

Roll some clay out of another colour on PM4, cut 2 pieces of 4cm x the height of the three canes. Cover both sides of each piece with the left over black/ white strips of clay made for the bullseye canes. Cover them white side towards the colour, black outside.

4

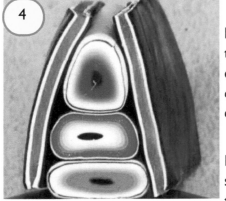

Place the two pieces either side of the three cane stack.

Flatten one side of the two remaining canes, and place either side of the two flat pieces, making a square shape.

5

Reduce the cane to around 1cm square and your cane is ready to use.

Cane 5 - vaneer:

6 Roll some scrap clay on PM5 I've used black so it shows better in the photograph.

Cut thin slices of the cane and place them end to end, matching the patterns - eg pink end to pink end, purple end to purple end.

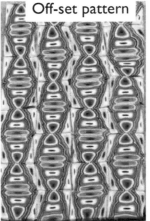

7

Lay the second layer of cane slices next to the first, but off-set. This gives the nice wavy line between the two helix patterns.
Once you've completed your vaneer, burnish as before.

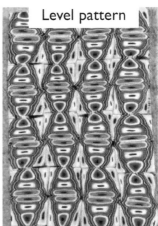

Off-set pattern

Level pattern

Random pattern

Graduated spots vaneer:

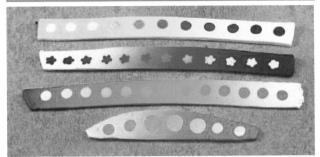

This breaks up the other vaneers with their busy patterns quite nicely. As you can see, the spots can be of the same colour as the background, or completely different.

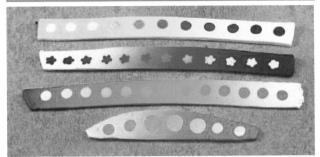

I've used different colours to demonstrate.

a. Roll clay on PM0 and cut one 3cm circle in while and the same in another colour.
b. Roll each circle into a log around 4cm long.
c. Fold both logs over, offsetting them as shown
d. Put through the pasta machine, then continue to fold and put through until you have a smooth blend.

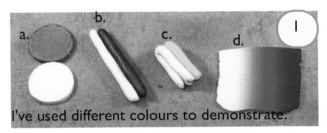

Once you have your blend, fold it over - as shown on the yellow clay - and put through the pasta machine lenghtways first on PM0, then PM2, and finally PM4.

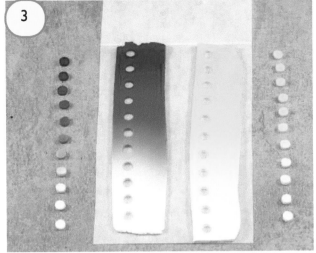

Place the blend on a piece of folded deli paper and cut 5mm holes as shown.

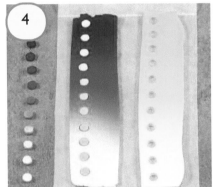

Put the cut out circles in the other piece of clay, starting with the dark circles of one colour in the light end of the other.

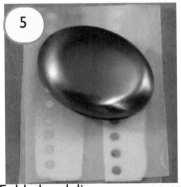
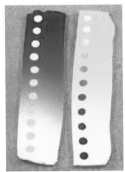

Fold the deli paper over and burnish the clay so that the circles are well joined to the clay and the surface is smooth.

Play about with various size circles, perhaps graduating in size, or other shapes such as hearts, stars or flowers.

Green/yellow stripes:

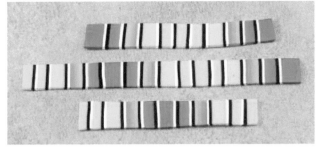

These can be in any colour, I just chose green and yellow as these were two colours I hadn't used much in the canes so far.

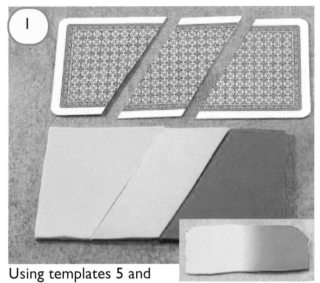

Using templates 5 and 6 as shown on the techniqes page 1, roll zinc yellow, wasabi and the green made from half peacock pearl and half wasabi clay on PM0. Make into a Skinner blend as shown on page 19.

Once you've got your blend, fold it in half as before, but this time put it through the pasta machine on PM0 with the short end first, making a longer, thinner blend. Then put it through again, short end first, on PM2, PM4 and PM6, ending up with a very long thin blend.

Now fold the blend back and forward in a fan fold, the width of 2cm, and you'll end up with what I call a plug. Start with eithr the yellow or green end.

Cut some black and white clay on PM0, 2cm x 4cm. Stack white on black.

Pinch one of the short 2cm ends and put through the pasta machine, short end first, on PM0, PM2, PM4 & PM6.

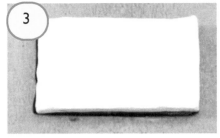

Take the green/yellow plug, and make 5 cuts at regular intervals as shown.

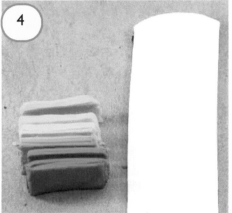

Insert the black/white clay in the five cuts. Make sure that the black/white strips are the same way up for each slice.

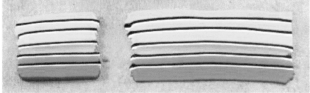

Cut a 5mm slice, then put through the pasta machine, stripes vertical, on PM0. PM2 and PM4. You can use it as it is, or cut equal size pieces and put them together as shown under the title.

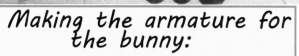

Making the armature for the bunny:

1

THE HEAD

3.5cm

4cm

Take some tin foil 30cm x 30cm and roll loosely into a ball. Next, gradually start to mould the ball into an egg shape, with a slightly pointed end, to measure 4cm x 3.5cm.

2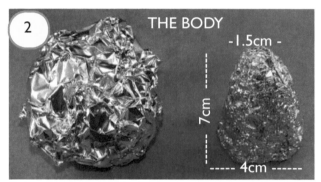

THE BODY

-1.5cm-

7cm

4cm

Take some tin foil 30cm x 60cm and roll loosely into a 8cm ball. Gradually start to mould the ball into a cone shape, 1.5cm at the top, 4cm at the bottom, and 7cm high.

3

Take 30cm x 15cm foil and wrap around the head and body.
Press well into the head and body to join the two peices.

4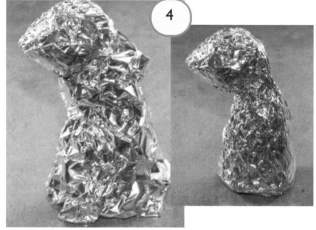

Continue adding more foil to the bunny until the head and body are securely joined.

As you can see, the basic shape is right, but the bunny needs to be fatter in its body.

5

Roll balls of foil loosely and press against the parts of the bunny you want to be fatter. Then press them into the body, shape, and cover with a sheet of foil to secure.

You might want to make the bunny cheeks fatter, it's the same method, just using smaller balls of foil.

Your bunny is now ready to cover with clay.

Making the armature for the chicken:

Take some foil 90cm x 30cm, roll loosely into a ball, then into a cone shape, but with the point to one side and more rounded on the other, as shown.

This shows the two bodies ready for adding the clay.

Covering with scrap clay:

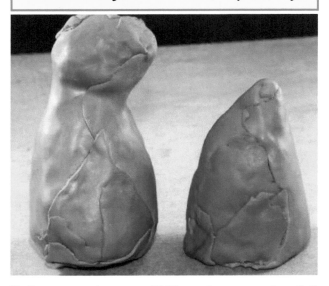

Roll scrap clay on PM2 and cover the foil shapes. Try not to overlap the clay as you only want one thickness all over. When covered, use a knitting needle or ball tool to blend all the joins so the clay is completely smooth - not shown above.

Making the bunny ears:

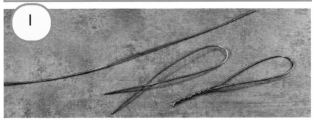

Cut some 1mm wire into 2 x 2cm pieces. Fold in half and 3cm from the ends, twist.

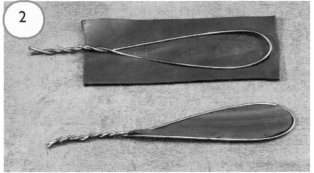

Roll some scrap clay on PM3 and cut a piece to fit inside the bunny ear. Repeat with the other ear wire.

Roll some pink clay and some white clay on PM0 and cut 2 x 3cm circles of each.

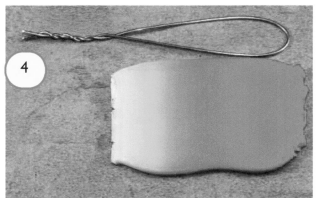

Follow steps 4 - 7 on page * to make a Skinner blend. Make sure that it's wide enough to cover the ears, the put it through the pasta machine (light end one side, dark the other) on PM0, PM2 and PM3

70

5

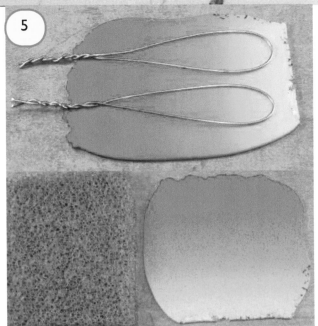

Make sure that both ears fit on the blend, then take a texture sheet of our choice and texture the pink blend. I like using this sponge which originally came from Lakeland, but equally good is using sand paper and running it through the pasta machine with the blend on PM0 setting. Put the pink blend to one side to use later.

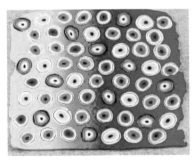

Decide which veneer you want to use for the outside of the bunny ears. I made up another one using the pattern below and making it into a Skinner blend then adding slices of the first canes you made in a random pattern.

6

Place your bunny ears on the <u>back</u> of the veneer and cut around 0.5cm wide all the way round.

7

Wrap round the ears as shown, covering the wire completely at first, then trimming off the excess flush with the wire.

8

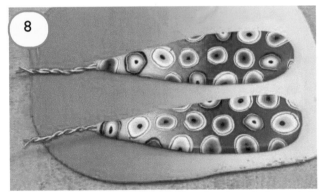

Now place the ears on the back of the pink blend (non textured side) and cut flush with the sides all the way round.

9

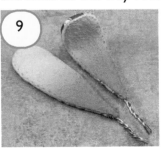

Press the edges down gently then if you want one floppy ear, bend it over. Finally make stitch marks with a needle took or 1mm ball tool.

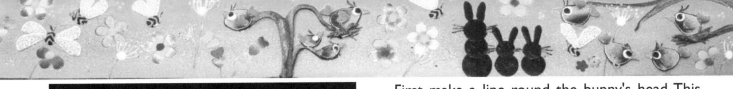

Showing one bunny with both ears straight, and one with one ear bent over.

Once you've decided on how you want your ears, cure them for 40 minutes at the clay manufacturer's recommended temperature. Either cure them on cornflower, or paper, so that you don't get any shiny parts.

Covering the bunny:

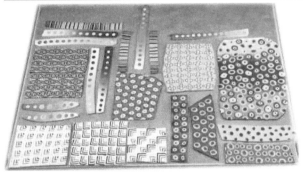

These are the veneers you've made, now it's time to put them on the bunny.

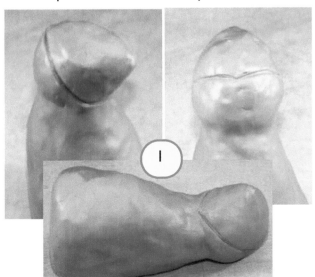

First make a line round the bunny's head. This line runs from the ears to under the chin, like a bonnet ribbon.

Cover the space betwen the lines, then cut two lines from pointed part (the nose) to the each side of the head as shown.

Fill in the part under the chin with a different veneer.

Take some strips of veneer, around 1cm wide, and put around the edges of the pieces you've already put in, then crossing them over like a bonnet ribbon underneath.

72

Continue to cover the head area of the bunny with patches of vaneer, cutting to shape as shown below.

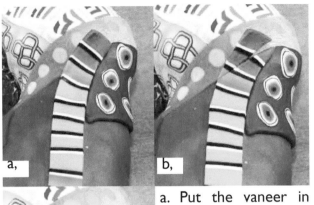

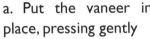

a. Put the vaneer in place, pressing gently

b. With a craft knife cut along the edge of where you want the vaneer to butt against

c. Press gently to fix into place. Finally, with a large knitting needle, burnish the join.

Make a two holes for the ears with a knitting needle, fill with polymer clay adhesive, I use Bake & Bond, and insert ears. For the nose, make a small log of clay into a V shape and place as shown. Insert the glass beads for eyes.

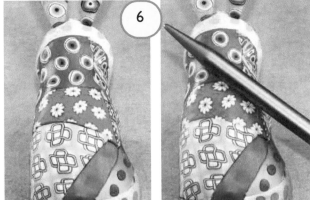

Continue covering the bunny with strips of vaneer, using the large knitting needle to join two pieces together as you go along.

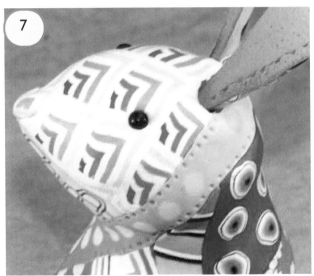

Once all the vaneers are on, to make the stitch marks use either a needle tool or a 1mm ball tool.

For the tail, roll some white clay into a ball and press onto the back of the bunny. With a ball tool make indentations all over.

Your bunny is now ready to be cured. Cure in the oven for 1 hour at the clay manufacturer's recommended temperature.

Finishing the bunny:

The last thing to do for your bunny is add the whiskers. To do this take a 2mm drill and make a hole either side of the bunny's face, where you want the whiskers to be. Make sure the two holes meet.

Put some superglue or similar into the hole and thread three strands of thin wire through the hole. Once dry, cut to size and separate.

Making the chicken beak, comb, wattle and feet:

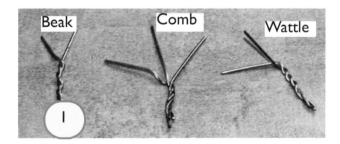

Beak   Comb   Wattle

1

Using 1mm wire, cut the following:
Beak: 2 x 4cm - twist 3cm
Comb: 3 x 4cm - twist 2cm
Wattle: 2 x 4cm - twist 2cm

2

Take some gold clay and roll a log 5mm diameter. Cut 2 x 1.5cm, round each end, then thread onto the beak wire, pressing the two ends together where they meet. For nostrils either make two holes with a needle tool or ball tool, or add two tiny balls of clay and make holes in them. Cure for 40 minutes.

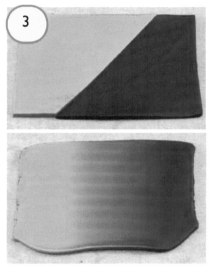

3

Roll gold clay and bronze clay on PM0 and cut a 9cm x 6cm rectangle out as you did for the spots cane. Make into a Skinner blend.

You now need to change the shape of you blend to this longer, thinner shape.

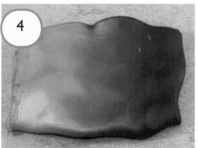

4

Fold your blend as you would before putting through the pasta machine again, but before you do, gently push the clay towards the middle, making it narrower. Do this all the way along the clay evenly, then put it through the pasta machine. Continue folding and narrowing until you have a strip that measures 3cm wide.

5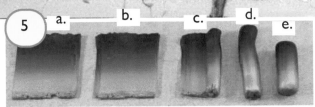

a.   b.   c.   d.   e.

Once you have a strip 3cm wide, put it through the pasta machine, narrow end first, on PM1 and PM3. You will now have a piece around 30cm long. Cut 13 x 2cm pieces.

a. The 2cm piece

b. Using your blade at an angle, cut a strip of clay off one end

c. Put the cut off piece at the other end of the clay and start rolling it up into a log

d. The completed log

e. Round the ends and shorten the log if required by rolling 'inwards'. This is opposite to the usual way you roll, bringing your hands towards each other as they roll.

6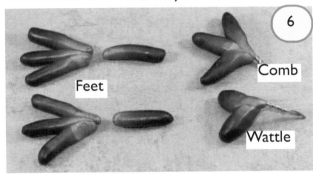

Feet

Comb

Wattle

Roll 8 of the logs to 3cm, these will be for the feet. Pinch three logs together at the gold ends, make two of these.

For the comb, reduce 3 logs to 2.5cm and thread onto the comb wire, pinching the gold ends together.

For the wattle reduce the remaining 2 logs to 2.5cm and thread onto the wattle wire, again pinching the gold ends. Cure the comb and wattle for 40 mins. Do not cure the feet.

To finish the feet, take any cutter, and using the non-cutting side make lines in each toe.

Covering the chicken:

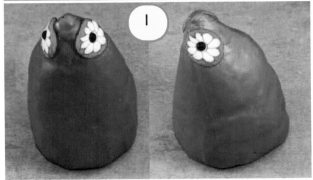

1

Start by placing two circular cane slices for the chicken's eyes. Place a 4mm black glass bead in the middle of each cane slice. Instead of a cane slice you could use circles of clay.

2

Cover the head area with the vaneers as explained in the 'covering the chicken' section. You only need to cover the area shown.

3

With a knitting needle make a hole in the middle of the face area where you want the beak to be. Put in some Bake & Bond or other clay adhesive and push in the beak.

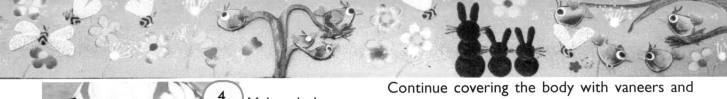

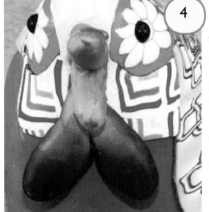

4 Make a hole with your needle tool and put in some clay adhesive. Push in the wattle so it fits underneath the beak.

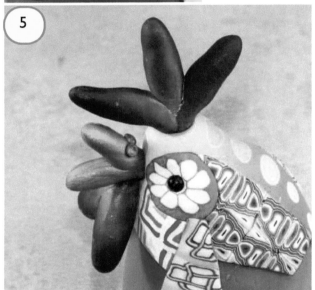

5

Finally make a hole with a knitting needle in the top of the chicken's head, put in some clay adhesive and push in the comb.

6

Continue covering the body with vaneers and follow the instructions in the 'covering the chicken' section on how to fit the vaneers together, burnish them and add the stitching. Put the feet on a tile and place the chicken on them, pressing down firmly to adhere.

7

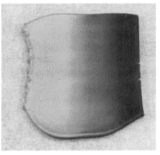

Roll some gold clay and some bronze clay on PM0 and cut 2 x 3cm circles of gold and 1 x 3cm circle of bronze. Overlap as shown, then put through the pasta machine on PM0. Fold and put through again, continue until you have a blend.

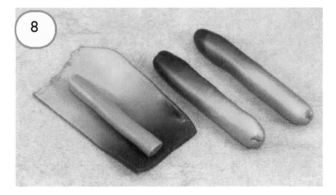

8

Put the blend through the pasta machine on PM2 and PM4, cut into three equal pieces. Roll some scrap clay and make three logs just a little smaller than the clay, wrap in the blended clay and round the two ends. The three logs should be 4cm long, so either lengthen or shorten them accordingly until you get to 4cm.

(9)

Decide which colours you want on the top, I chose to have alternative bronze, gold, bronze, pinch the bottom of all three together and press firmly onto the chicken. Finally use the non-cutting side of a metal cutter to make the lines. Your chicken is now ready to cure.

Cure for an hour at the clay manufacturer's recommended temerature. Once cool varnish if you want a shiny chicken, I use Darwi Vernis.

What a fantastic group of people I met in Ireland when I taught the patchwork bunnies and chickens. Here are some photos of the weekend. I don't think I've ever laughed so much!

Angela Kent

Sophie Barry's bunny. Sophie was aged 11. A very talented girl.

Laura Barry's bunny.

Margaret O'Neill and Rosemary Stafford

Celine Neenan and Pauline Dunleavy

Dell O'Leary   Tina Kapahnke

Pauline Dunleavy

Niamh Coulter's bunny

77

Pat the flat cow:

& her flatmates!

I visited someone once and saw a strange model of a metal flat cow with a wobbly head. I liked the idea of having a flat model as it's rare that we look at the back of our creations and these stand nicely against a wall. I've played about with doing zentangles in clay, and the flat surface of cow is the perfect canvas!

TOOLS & MATERIALS:

- Pasta machine
- Tissue blade
- Craft knife • Ruler
- Oven to cure clay in
- Tile to work on
- Acrylic or metal clay roller
- Needle tool / cocktail stick
- Deli wrap
- Wire cutters
- Soap stone for burnishing – or a smooth stone. bone folder or credit card can also be used
- 2 wooden kebab skewers. each around 25cm long and 3–4mm in diameter
- 1mm wire – 8cm piece – I buy this from the garden centre
- Cardboard 10cm x 10cm x 2
- Pen and pencil
- Scissors
- Wet wipes (baby wipes)
- Polymer clay adhesive eg Bake & Bond. but any will do
- Polymer clay varnish. I use Darwi Vernis gloss

CUTTERS:

- Circle cutters 4cm. 3cm. 2cm. 7mm & 5mm. I also use Ferrule bootlace crimps in 4mm.2mm & 1mm – find a friendly electrician who will have lots!! (so do Ebay) These crimps are great as they come in a variety of sizes

- Oval cutters. you can use any size but I use
  - 12mm x 1cm
  - 12mm x 7mm
  - 7mm x 4mm

- Leaf cutter around 2.25mm x 1cm – optional. you can use a craft knife to cut the ears

Ferrule bootlace crimps

CLAY:

- 3 x 56g blocks of white clay
- 1 x 56g block of black clay

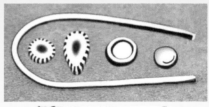

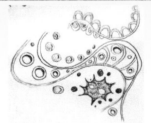

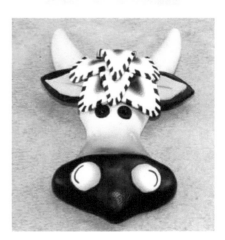

Making the hooves, legs and tail:

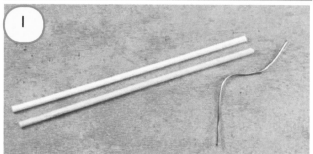

Cut 12cm off each kebab skewer from the non-pointed end. Keep the remaining pieces, you'll need them later. Bend the piece of 8cm wire as shown, with 4cm of straight wire which will be embeded into the cow, and the rest bent in whatever shape you want the tail to be.

Roll 2 x 3cm circles on PM0 with black clay, roll them into a ball, then into a dome. Finally push the dome into a teardrop shape. The photo on the right is the underside of the two hooves which shows the shape.

Roll 2 x 3cm circles on PM0 of black and white clay. Cut each circle in half, making 8 halves, and roll each piece into a 6cm log. Line the logs up alternating the black and white.

Gently roll the logs to adhere, then put them through the pasta machine on PM0.

Place the kebab stick on the end and roll round.

Cut leaving a gap as shown.

It is important to leave a gap as the stripes need to be tight against the stick. You can easily close the gap by gently pushing the two sides together.

Use a knitting needle or ball tool to roll the seam so it's smooth. Don't roll it as this will stretch the stripy clay and it will become loose and distorted.

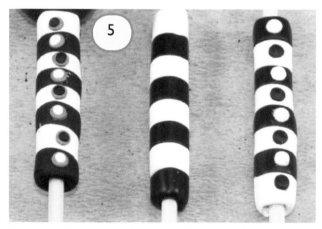

You can leave the legs as they are (middle), or roll black and white clay on PM6 and cut 4mm circles (right). For the leg on the left, I've rolled grey clay on PM6 and cut 4mm circles, then put 2mm black and white circles on top.

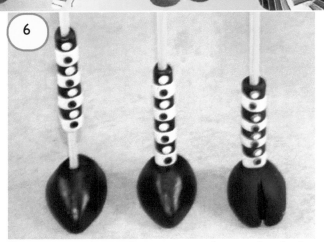

6

Put some clay adhesive on the end of the kebab stick and insert the stick into the hoof. Push the stripy leg down to touch the hoof. Finally make a cut with your needle tool in the middle of the front of the hoof, and push a little apart. The legs are now ready for curing.

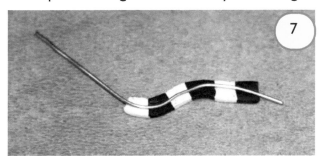

7

For the tail take the remaining piece of stripy clay and roll it on PM2, making sure that the stripes are vertical - you want them longer, not wider. Cut a strip 1/2cm wide, and remove one black section and one white section, leaving 6. Push the curved part of the wire into the stripy clay, leaving around 1cm uncovered at the end. Gently press the clay round to cover the wire.

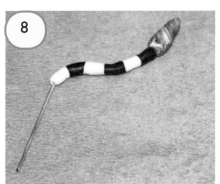

8

To finish, roll a small ball of grey clay and put on the end of the wire, tapering the clay as shown.

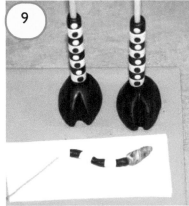

9

Put the hooves flat on a small tile to cure, and the tail on a piece of paper. Cure for 1 hour at the clay manufacturers recommended temperature.

It's really important that you make sure that your legs are upright, not leaning sideways, backwards or forwards, as they have to hold the whole cow, and if they're not straight, they're likely to be unstable.

Zentangle canes:

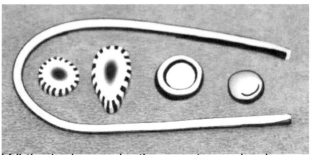

While the legs and tail are curing, make the zentangle canes.

3D circle:

80

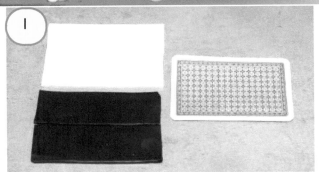

1

Roll some black clay and some white clay on PM0 and cut out the size of a standard playing card (9cm x 6cm). Cut each piece in half as shown above.

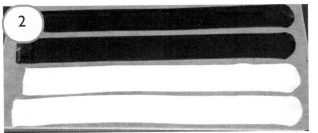

2

Lengthen each strip by putting through the pasta machine on PM2, PM4, then PM6. On ONE of the black strips, put through on PM8 as well, making a longer and thinner strip.

3

Taking one of the white strips of clay, cut 2cm off one end.

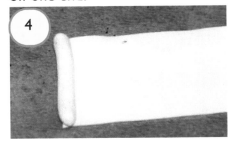

4

Roll the cut off piece of clay into a log and place at the end of the strip.

Now roll up to make a cane. Rolling up the clay in this way prevents you getting a little hole in the middle of the cane.

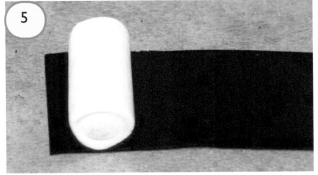

5

Taking the black strip that's been rolled to PM8, lay the white cane on it and cut a straight line to one side.

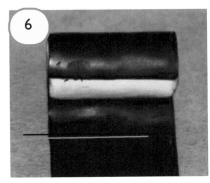

6

Roll the black clay all the way round the log and a little further, then when you roll it back again there will be a faint line.

It didn't show well on the photo so I've put a light blue line where it is. Cut along the line

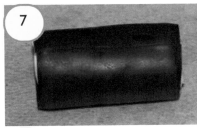

7

and the black clay should join seamlessly. Gently roll to remove the join.

8

We're now going to make the 'shadow' part of the cane. With the PM8 black strip, cut the following four pieces:
4cm, 3.5cm, 3cm, 2.5cm
With your finger, gently press down on the two side edges to make them thinner.

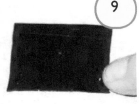

9

10 Starting with the larger piece, 4cm, lay it round the cane. Then put the 3.5cm piece on top, in the middle of the 4cm piece, with equal size gap each side. Continue with the other two pieces. Once all

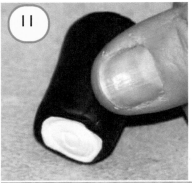

11 Once all four pieces are on, with your finger or thumb gently stroke across the edges to make sure there are no ridges or steps.

The cane slice on the left is made as instructed, making sure the edges of the four pieces making up the shadow were thinner and using the black strip of PM8 thickness.

The cane slice on the right was made using black on PM6, and without thinning the edges. Needless to say I will not be using that one!

Shadow circle:

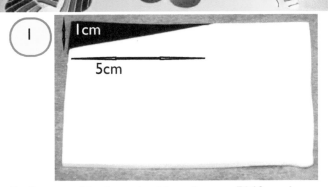

1 1cm / 5cm

Roll some black and white clay on PM0 and cut a playing card size. The black part is 1cm deep and 5cm long.

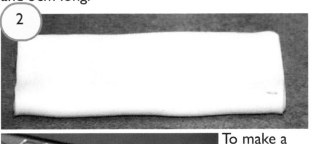

2

To make a Skiinner blend, fold the clay in half and put through the pasta machine, folded part downwards. Keep folding, always with the black edge one side and the white edge the other. I swap the clay round every turn, black on left, then black on right, to keep it more even as the rollers are slightly closer together nearer the edge.

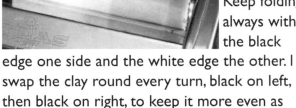

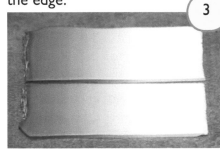

3 Once you have a smooth blend, cut it in half as shown.

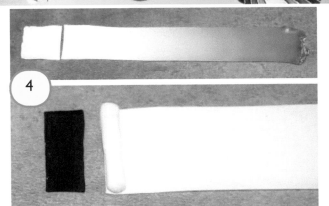

Take one of the halves and roll out on PM2, PM4 and PM6. Cut 3cm off the white end and roll this into a log. Place at the end of the strip. Take some black clay on PM6 and cut a 1cm strip; with your finger, gently press the two long edges as you did in the previous cane.

Continue adding pieces of the strip to the cane, making each new piece slightly shorter than the previous one, and smoothing down each time. To finish, cover with black clay on PM8 and roll to 7cm long.

Roll the white strip once round the log, then place the 1cm strip of black clay on top, pressing down gently to adhere.

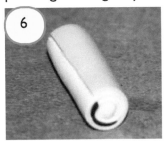

Stripy bullseye:

Continue rolling until the grey appears, then cut it off level with the end of the black piece. With your finger smooth down the edge, then place the remaining strip the other side, again in line with the black and smoothing down the join.

Roll some white and black clay on PM2, the size of a standard playing card, with the black part being 2.5cm along the top, and tapering to the bottom right corner.

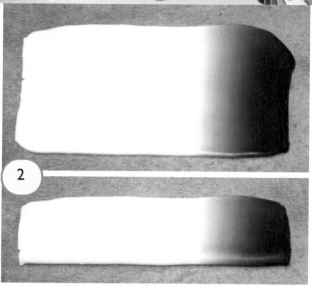

Cut 6 x 3mm slices off the stack, then put them through the pasta machine on PM0. This just ensures that they are all of an even width just incase your cutting isn't exact - mine isn't!

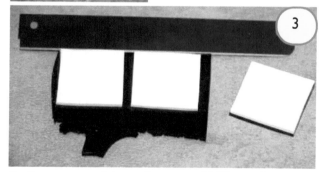

Make into a Skinner blend, fold in half, put through the pasta machine lengthways on PM2, PM4 & PM6, then roll up with the black end in first. Roll so the cane is 3cm high.

There are two ways of covering the cane. You can either lay the pieces side by side as shown above, roll gently with your roller to stick them together, cut a straight edge then wrap around the cane. Or you can cut a straight edge on each individual piece and lay it on the cane, trimming to size as you go.

Roll some white clay on PM2 and cut 3 squares, 3cm x 3cm each. Roll some black clay also on PM2, place the white square on it and cut round them.

Stack the squares, alternating black and white, then make 3mm marks on the top square. I use a Marxit tool, but a ruler works too.

I usually use the second method as I find it easier to trim the smaller pieces. When all covered, roll to 1.5cm diameter, cut in half and roll the other half to 1cm diameter. Take the 1.5cm half and pinch one side to make a leaf shape.

84

Long edging strip:

Roll some white clay on PM0 and cut 12cm x 3cm. Cover both sides with black on PM8. Put through the pasta machine lengthways on PM0 and your edging strip is done. This is a very useful way of defining shapes on your zentangle pattern.

Designing Pat:

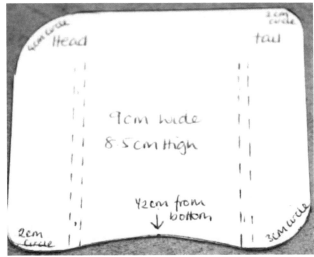

First make your pattern. I make this in cardboard as it's easier to cut round later. Cut a rectangle 9cm x 8.5cm. Using a 4cm circle cutter, make a curve on the top left corner. Using a 3cm circle cutter make a curve on the bottom right corner, and with a 2cm circle cutter, make curved corners in the bottom left and top right corners. You obviously don't need to use cutters, circles cut in cardboard work just as well.

For the bottom curve, find the middle of the bottom edge and mark it. Then mark 0.5cm up from the mark. Make a nice curve from the corner up to the middle mark, and back to the corner. The middle of the dotted lines are 2cm from each side. These mark where the legs go.

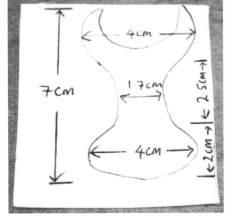

For the head follow the diagram on the left. First make a rectangle 7cm x 4cm, and then put in the rest of the dimensions.

Cut both the body and the head out in cardboard ready to make the design. Then draw round the carboard body, and also put the head in the right place and draw round it. This gives you an idea of where the head is going to be so you know which part of your design will be visible. Below are some designs I drew, but have fun, be creative, play!

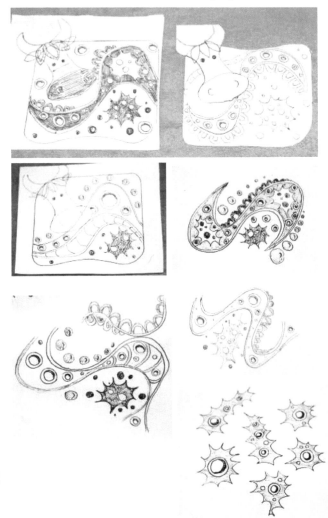

85

This is the design I'm going with.

Making the head:

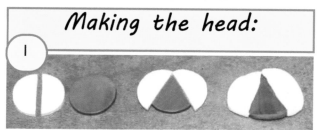

To make the horns, cut I x 3cm circle on PM0 and I x 3cm circle on grey. To make the grey just blend together some of the scraps of white and black clay you have. Cut the white circle in half, and place the two halves either side of the grey circle as shown. Put throught the pasta machine on PM0.

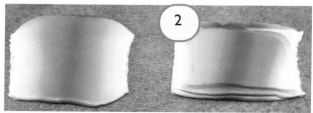

Once you have a nice blend (picture on the left), use your blade to make a bevelled edge on the top or bottom side.
The piece you've cut off, place on the bottom edge, as shown in the picture on the right.
Making a thinner edge makes a better, less noticable join when you roll it up.

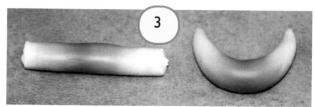

Roll up the blend, from the bottom edge, then round both ends by pulling the outside edges inwards to make a smooth end. Finally make the tube pointed at each end, thicker in the middle, and 6cm long. Curve round to the shape of the horns on your cardboard template.

For the head you need 2 x 3cm circles on PM0. I've used one grey and one white, however I like 1.5 white and 0.5 grey best. Overlap the circles and put through the pasta machine on PM0, folding and putting through until you have a blend. Cut a piece off at an angle as you did for the horns and roll up. Round both ends.

Take your log and shorten it to 2.5cm. Do this by rolling it and bringing your hands towards each other rather than away, this will make it shorter and thicker. To fit the head onto the horns, press each end of the head part, and the front middle of the horns, and push the grey end of the head onto the horns.

For the muzzle, roll 2 x 3cm circles of black clay on PM0, roll them together and make into an oval shape 4cm wide, with a little 'v' shape in the middle of the bottom edge. Place this on the thin part of the head.

7

To make the ears, roll some black clay on PM2 and cut two leaf shapes, around 2.25cm x just over 1cm. I have a handy cutter this size, but you can draw the shape and cut it out in cardboard, then use this as a template. Roll some light grey clay on PM6 and cut two more, the same size. Then with your craft knife, cut a little off the grey shapes, and place this on the black clay. To finish, using a needle tool or thin knitting needle, make a line down the middle, and gently pinch the bottom end.

8

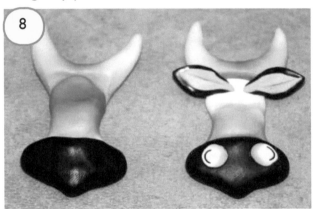

Place the muzzle on the head, then the two ears as shown, just overlapping the bottom of the horns. For the nostrils I've used thin slices of the shadow circle cane.

9

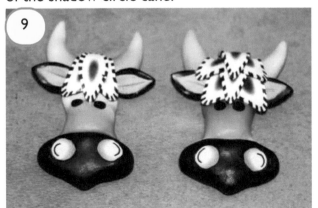

For the eyes roll black clay on PM4 and cut 2 x 5mm circles. Place on the head, and make a tiny hole with a needle tool in the middle of each.

Take the 1.5cm diameter stripy bullseye cane and pinch one end to make a leaf shape. Cut 6 slices and put three on the head, with the middle one the third one you place. Repeat with the other three, slightly higher up than the first, and press down gently to adhere.

Keep using the template to make sure the head is the right size.

The head part on the right was made using 1/2 circle grey and 1.5 circles in white.

Making the zentangle pattern - starting with the splodge:

1

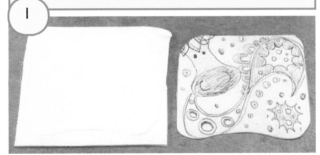

Once you've chosen your design, put it on cardboard and cut to size. Roll some white clay on PM3 and cut a piece slightly larger than the cow body shape. Make a light mark where the shape is so you can see where to put the designs.

87

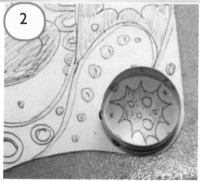

2

We're going to start with the pattern that looks like a paint splat! Take a cutter that just goes round the shape. This is a 3cm circle.

Roll some black clay on PM3 and cut out a 3cm circle - or whichever cutter you've used. Also roll some white clay on PM3.

Take an oval cutter, I've used two sizes: 11mm x 7mm and 12mm x 1cm. Cut a piece of deli paer, fold in half, and place the clay on it. This makes it much easier to make the design without distorting it

3

Using the oval cutters, cut half-ovals all the way round the circle. Then cut the same size ovals in white clay and insert them in the holes.

4

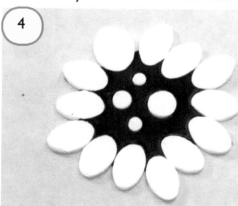

Continue all the way round. I've also put some circles in the middle.

5

Fold the deli paper over, and using a soap stone, a bone tool or a credit card, rub gently all over to 'burnish' the clay, which basically means making all the joins smooth and even.

6

Finally, using the original cutter you used, cut round your design.

7

Look to see where the splodge is going to be on the design, and cut out the shape in the right place.

8

Put the circle of splodge in the hole, and burnish to remove the joins. It now looks like it's just appeared there!

In-laying swirls and arches:

You're now going to make the swirl; this is fiddly, so first cut out the swirl from your cardboard template and put onto your clay in the place you want it to be.

Using your craft knife, cut round the shape and remove the white clay. Put it to one side, you're going to need it later.

As the top half of the swirl is black, roll out black clay on PM3 and cut a piece slightly larger than the design.
Taking your pre-made white splodge, insert it as before in the black clay. Burnish well.

Cut out to the correct size using your cardboard template.

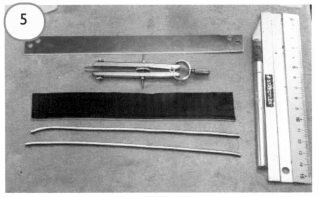

Next you have to cut a strip from the edging cane. First measure the thickness of PM3 on your machine, on my Atlas this is 2mm. Cut a strip to the same width.

First make a mark 2mm along the long side, the easiest way to do this is use a double pointed compass - shown above the cane, but you can use a ruler.

Then with a long blade (I use a 19cm blade), you can cut straight down, or use a ruler and craft knife.

Make a mark all the way round your shape, the same width as the piece of edging you've cut.

The double ended compass is very good for this. Then cut the strip off and place your edging strip round.

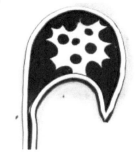

89

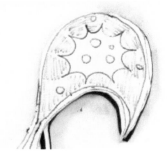

Keep checking with your cardboard pattern that your clay is the right size.

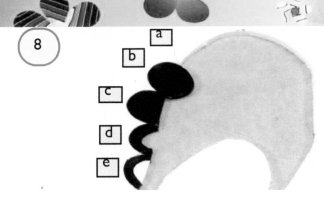

⑧

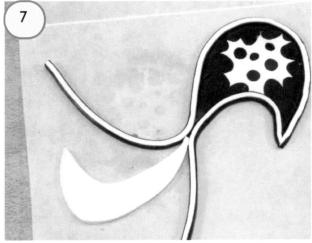

⑦

a. using an oval cutter, cut out an arch shape
b. remove the white clay, cut the same size oval in black clay PM3 and insert
c. burnish gently, then using your craft knife, trim the excess black clay
d. with a smaller oval cutter, make another cut
e. cut the same size oval in white clay PM3, and insert. Burnish and trim as before.

Now complete the rest of the swirl by putting the white part in, again cutting a strip off all the way round to accommodate the edging strip.

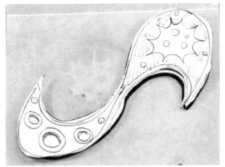

Again, check with the cardboard pattern that it's the right size.

The finished arches.

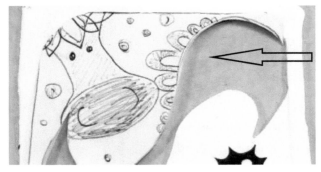

Before you put the swirl back in, you're going to make the arches which line the swirl.

⑨

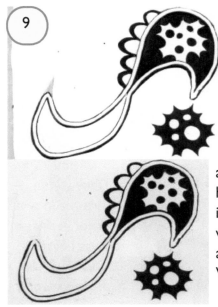

To finish, replace the swirl. Despite all your checking, it can still not fit, or as shown here, has a gap. This is easily filled with white clay and burnished. Voila, no gap!

Adding spots:

Cut thin slices of whichever circle cane you want to use. It's unlikely you're going to be able to cut perfect circles, so press them gently onto the tile, and with your blade, push them into a circle again.

Rather than burnishing, which can distort the circle, cover with deli wrap and press down directly onto the circle. This will embed it into the clay without changing its shape. If you want a really smooth cow, you can then burnish, but I prefer to have better circles.

Use your cardboard head shape and place it on the body so you can see where you want to put the remaining spots.

The finished design.

Putting it all together:

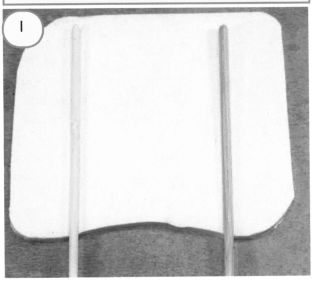

Roll some white clay on PM0 and cut the body shape. Using the off-cuts from the wooden skewers, place them 2cm from each side.

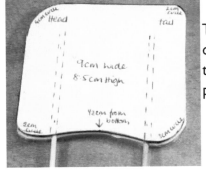

The dotted lines denote where the legs will be placed.

91

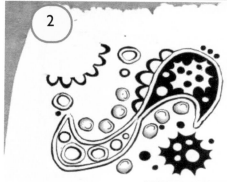

2

Roll some white clay on PM2, lay the design on it, press down and cut out the body shape.

3

Put some clay adhesive on the wire part of the tail and put in place on the same piece of clay that you put the leg sticks.

4

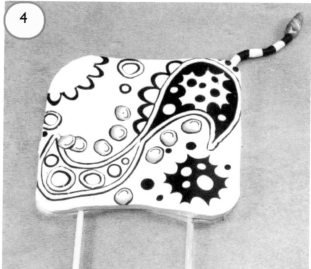

Place the two pieces of body together, sandwiching the leg sticks and tail between them.

5

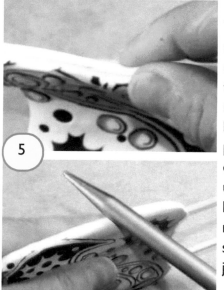

You now need to smooth all the way round the body. First pinch the edge, then I use a large knitting needle to smooth the join.

To add the head, first put some clay adhesive on the back of the head, not the tips of the horns, and place on the body where you want it to be.

6

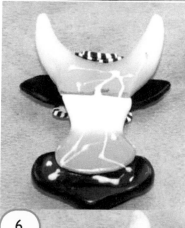

7

Put some clay adhesive on the wooden parts of the legs.

8

Take out the off-cut wooden sticks and insert the legs. I like to use a wet wipe at this point to clean up the body and remove any smudges in grey or black. You can lightly sand after curing for any more stubborn marks. Pat is now ready for curing.

9

Your cow needs to be supported to cure otherwise she'll fall over. I use a coffee pod box, and kitchen roll loosely scrunched to stop her moving. Cure at the clay manufacturer's recommended temperature for one hour, in a pre-heated oven. Leave to cool then varnish.

Leather effect blade cases and hair barrettes:

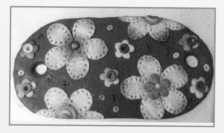

TOOLS & MATERIALS:

- Pasta machine   • Ruler
- Tissue blade
- Craft knife
- Oven to cure clay in
- Tile to work on
- Acrylic or metal clay roller
- Needle tool / cocktail stick
- Extruder with 1mm circle hole
- Wooden kebab skewer
- Ball tools, 1mm and 2mm
- Small flat screwdriver approx 2mm wide
- Dentist tool (optional)
- Texture sheet, or roller (optional)
- Circle cutters 3cm, 1cm and various smaller ones – I use Ferrule bootlace crimps
- Baby wipe
- Self-adhesive magnetic tape

CLAY:

For each blade case:

- Two blocks of Fimo Leather Effect clay for the two sides of the case. If you want a graduated blend, use 4 x 1/2 blocks of the colours of your choice

- Around 1/4 x 56g block of white clay, not leather effect

- Around 1/4 x 56g block of black or dark brown clay, not leather effect

- Small amounts of other colours of Fimo leather effect clay for the decorations

Making the blade case body:

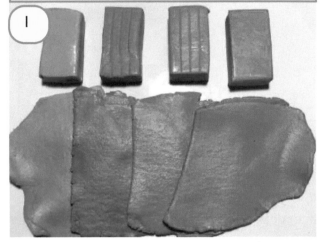

If you want a graduated colour for your background, take four x 1/2 blocks of clay. If you only want the one colour, use two blocks. Put the clay through the pasta machine on PM0

Squish the clay into the shapes above. The two middle colours will be triangles and the two outside colours will be half triangles. In order to get a little bit of the true colours, make sure that the shapes allow for each colour to have a little part where it's not mixing with another colour.

Here:

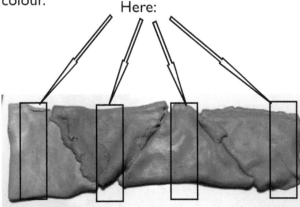

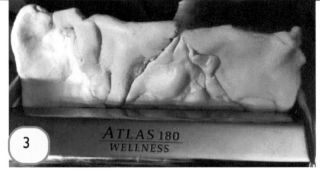

Leather effect clay is more difficult to make into a blend compared to other clay as it's very soft, so it's easier when making a large blend to make it the width of your pasta machine.

Continue as you would for making any Skinner blend, not worrying if it comes out mishappen, it's very malleable, it can be eased back into the correct shape easily.   Once blended, for the case roll out on PM1.

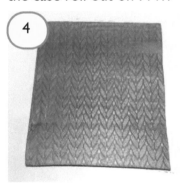

I like to texture the inside of my blace case, and in this case used a sugarcraft roller as it's the width of the clay. However, you can use any texture you like.

You could also make your own as I've done here on the left of the picture, making the marks and filling them in once cured with acrylic paint. The picture on the right shows the plait texture filled in with acrylic paint after curing. Texturing is optional.

5

You're now going to cut out two pieces, one for the front of the blade case and one for the back. In the photo above I've cut just the one piece, then cut it in half, but it's much easier to cut 2 rectangles, each measuring 15cm x 6.5cm. Notice how I'm using the clay blade, more like a craft knife rather than cutting straight down.

Picture on the left showing that you can use just one large piece and fold it over as a different design.

One of the things that makes this clay so realistic looking are the little fibres in it. However, this makes cutting difficult, so use either a craft knife to cut, or the end of your blade, like a knife. Cutting this way makes a better cut and you can usually cut the clay in one go.

Even using a craft knife, you won't get a clean cut (right hand half). Go over again with your blade or knife, cutting off the little fibres (left hand half) to make a neater edge.

6

Once you've cut your pieces, the fun starts! I love love love designing these. Take some paper and draw out rectangles 15cm x 6.5cm and play about with designs until you've something you'd like to use on the blade case.

7

Cut out the designs in paper and arrange them on the clay.

This makes it easier to position them exactly where you want them.

Roll the leather clay for the decorations on PM6 and cut the shapes using the paper templates.

8

Add details such as the eyes, nose etc on top of the basic shape.

9 The finished front.

For the stitch effect found the dogs' heads I've used a very small ball tool, although you could equally use a needle tool or cocktail stick.

The bones have diagonal stiching. As a saddler I used to stitch using two needles and thread, and made stitch marks with a metal tool with diagonal teeth.

I show how imitate this stitching on the photo of a hair barette below.

10

First, using a 2mm wide screwdriver, or any tool that makes a 2mm line, make regularly spaced diagonal lines.

Using an extruder with a 1mm attachment, put whatever coloured clay you want to use, making sure that it is NOT the leather effect clay as this clay doesn't make nice clean 'thread' due to the fibres in it.
Cut around 2mm pieces and place in the opposite diagonal to the first marks.

Finish by pushing down to adhere and cure the two pieces for 1 hour at 130° C

Making the hinges:

11

Roll some leather clay on PM3 and cut out 6 pieces 3.3cm x 1.25cm. Make stitch marks along the two long sides of each piece, and fold round a wooden skewer, pressing the ends together and pinching the end slightly to reduce the thickness.

12

Keeping the hinges on the skewer, put them alternatively, three on each piece, equally spaced. Put some polymer clay adhesive on the part of the hinges attaching to the case sides; I use Kato Polyclay or Genesis Thick Medium Extender. Cure for 60 minutes at 130°C.
Once cured, cut two pieces of magnetic tape and place on the right side inside the case.

Your blades will attach safely to the magnetic tape.

Hair Barrettes:

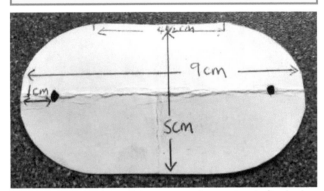

This is the size of barrette I made. I find the easiest way to make templates with rounded corners is to cut the rectangle to the size you want - in this case 9cm x 5cm - then fold it twice, once lengthways, once widthways. You can then cut all four corners in one go, ensuring that they are all exactly the same. I roll out the clay on PM2 for the hair barrettes.

Leaves:

As this clay doesn't mix in the same way as traditional polymer clay, I find that the best way to get a lovely watercolour effect of colours is to chop it up. Take small amounts of the colours you want and chop them up quite finely with your blade. Then put through the pasta machine on setting 6.

I've shown setting 5 in the picture, ignore that and put through on 6

Tear up the thin sheet into smaller pieces and put through the pasta machine once more, again on PM6. If you're happy with the blend, cut out a leaf shape, if you'd like more blend, repeat the tearing up stage.

I've used a needle tool to make a mark down the middle of the leaf to look like a vein.

Roll two colours out on PM6 and cut different size circles. I've used 6mm and 4mm on the darker clay and 4mm and 3mm on the green . Place them on the leaf and press down gently. Finally I made more vein marks, and used a

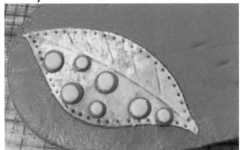

1mm ball tool to make stitch marks round the edge.

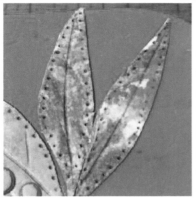

For these leaves I've used a different combination of colours and cut two longer leaves. I've just put the middle vein mark in and the stitch marks.

For this leaf I've rolled blue and yellow clay on PM6 and cut out circles, cut them in half and put round the edge of the leaf.

The vein in the middle is a thin rolled log of clay, it might have been better to have used 1mm extruded clay instead. I've also make little indentation with a ball tool just to add texture.

To finish I've used a needle tool to make grasses which will be back-filled with clay once cured. I've also put in two holes for the wooden rod to go through, 1cm from each end. Finally, no leaf is complete without a ladybird or two!

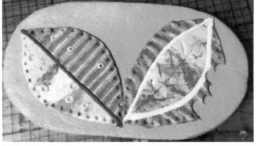

We're now going to make these leaves, starting with making the stripy part.

Roll three colours out on PM0 and cut a 3cm circle of each colour. Overlap by about a third, as shown in the left of the picture, then put through the pasta machine, still on PM0. Fold and repeat until you have a blend.

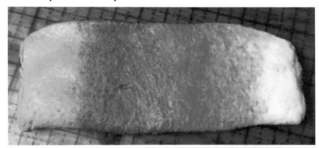

Once the clay is blended, fold it in half widthways, then put through the pasta machine lengthways, the smalled side first. Put through again on PM2, PM4 and PM6 until you have a long thin strip. Fold this up in a fan fold around 2cm wide.

You will have made this plug of clay.

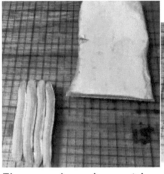 

Flatten the plug with your roller, keeping it 2-3cm wide until it's 4mm thick. Cut thin slices off and lay them side by side. Finish by rolling them gently with your polymer clay roller then putting through the pasta machine on PM6, with the stripes running vertically. This is important as you don't want the stripes any wider.

Make a blended veneer as you did for the first leaf, rolled on PM6. Roll some brown clay on PM6

Roll some brown clay on PM6 and cut a thin strip to sandwich between the two pieces.

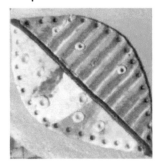

Then cut a leaf shape. I've finished it by adding small yellow balls and making stitch marks.

I've made another leaf using the two veneers, cutting out some 'bites' from the second leaf, and adding stitching.

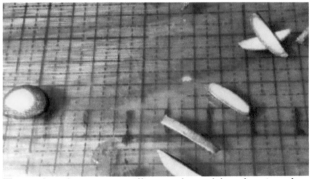

To make the catterpillar, make a blend using 1 x 3cm circle of green clay and 1/2 a 3cm circle of green clay, then make into a bullseye cane. Cut slices off the cane, it will automatically squash down, pulling one back into a circle for the head and the others into half moon shapes.

Don't forget to put the holes in for the skewer

To cure, put the barrette on something rounded like a coffee tin or glass and cure for 60 minutes at 130° C.

100

Making flower petals:

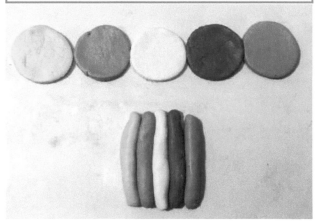

To make the blends for the flower petals, cut 3cm circles on PM0 in the required colours, then roll into logs. Roll with your roller so the logs stick together then put through the pasta machine on PM0.

Fold as shown and put through again. Repeat until it is the required blend. This clay can be challenging to blend as it's so soft.

It's very likely to come out of the pasta machine mishapen. In which case, fold it as before the squish it inwards until it's even (picture on the right). When you put it through the pasta machine the next time, push it firmly against one end of the machine, this will help it keep its shape.

Put the blend through the pasta machine on PM2, PM4 & PM6, with the stripes running vertically.

You want a long thin blend so you get several flower petals out of it.

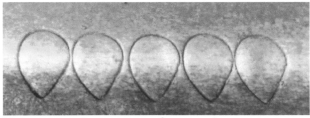

Using a petal cutter, cut five petals.

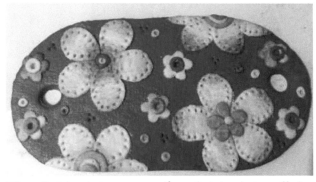

The finished barrette. I've finished it off by adding centres to the flower, smaller flowers cut using a small flower cutter, and stitch marks around just the large petals.

Once you've cured the piece you can decide whether you want to back-fill the stich marks. See the following page for how to do this. I think for this barrette I left them un-filled.

To back-fill with clay:

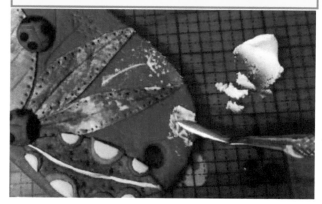

Back-filling involves making marks in clay before curing, then filling in with clay once the piece is cured. It allows you to make thin lines or designs in your clay. I use this technique a lot in my designs, it can add little details, like the grasses in this piece, which would be difficult to make using little bits of raw clay.

To do, take the colour you wish to use and make it as soft as possible. I use a dentist tool to push the clay into the holes and lines.

Once all is filled, use your tool to scrape off any excess clay.

Use a wet wipe to remove the remaining excess clay and cure for 15 minutes at 130° C.

GALLERY:

Steampunk dragonfly pendants:

CLAY:	I've used Premo gold, silver and copper clay, but any metallic clay will work. For the middle pendant I've also used a little purple for the dragonfly wings. You can use any extra colours you wish.

TOOLS & MATERIALS:

- Pasta machine
- An oven to cure clay in
- Tile to work on
- Clay cutting blade
- Craft knife
- Needle tool or cocktail sticks
- 6cm and 1cm diameter circle cutters
- A metal bowl to cure the pendants on. I buy them from Ikea for about £2, but you can use a bath bomb mould, or anthing that has a curve such as a round glass vase or basin.
- Some card to make a dragonfly wing templat
- Pencil and scissors
- 80 or 100 grit wet & dry sandpaper
- A marker pen such as a sharpie
- Black acrylic paint and paint brush
- Kitchen towel and wet wipes
- Tin foil
- Cotton buds
- Gilder paste. I've used silver, gold and bronze
- Varnish. I use Darwi Vernis
- Choker wires. I buy 18" length ones

FOR TEXTURE & DECORATION:

- I use Ferrule bootlace crimps – find a friendly electrician who will have lots, or I buy them from ebay. These are great as they come in a variety of sizes and can also be made into other shapes. The ones I used in this tutorial are 6mm, 5mm, 4mm & 3mm.

- A small teardrop cutter can be made by taking a 5mm bootlace crimp and, with a pair of pliers, squeezing one side to a point.
- Various tools to make texture with, such as a ball tool, a dentist tool, sculpture tools, screwdriver bits etc
- Texture makers for the pendant background: MKM rollers, Kor rollers, plastic packaging that has a pattern on it, lace, hessian, string, buttons, the list is endless
- A zip mould or zip
- Thin wire

Making the back of the pendants:

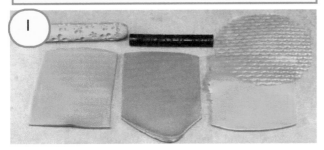

Roll out the gold, silver and copper clay on PM2, around 7cm square. Decide what texture you want on each pendant. I've used a MKM flower roller on the gold, a Kor dragonfly roller on the silver, and some plastic that was part of a food container on the copper. You can use anything for texture, lace is lovely, it's not necessary to buy expensive rollers, but they do make a lovely background.

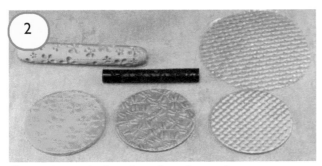

Cut a 6cm circle of each colour clay.

Carefully press the circles onto a bowl, making sure that the edges are touching the bowls. If not pressed down firmly they may lift, giving you an uneven edge.

Using a 12mm or 1cm circle cutter, cut two holes in each clay circle and remove the middles with your needle tool. Put the two holes around 1cm from the edge, and in the top half of the circle.

Pre-heat the oven to the clay manufacturers recommended temperature and cure for one hour. It is important to cure them for this length of time as they need to be strong.

Making the front of the pendants:

Roll the clay on PM2, and texture and cut three circles, exactly as you did for the backs.

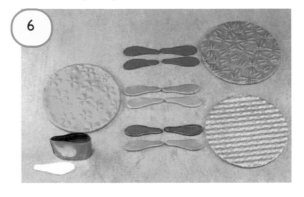

To make the wings, either cut a wing shape in cardboard as a guide, or I've squashed a 2cm circle cutter to a wing shape, useful if you're making as many as I did!

Roll the clay on PM5 and cut 4 wings for each dragonfly. You can texture the clay before cutting if you want a textured wing. Don't be limited to the same colour for all wings, I like making two in one colour and two in another.

Lay the wings on the circles as shown, press down gently.

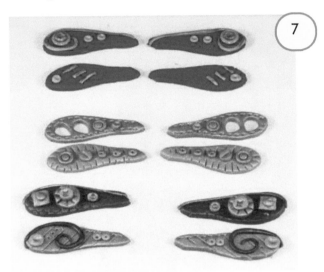

Texture and decorate three sets of wings. There really are no rules for this, be as creative, as elaborate or as simple as you wish. Below are some tiles that I made of examples of steampunk decorations.

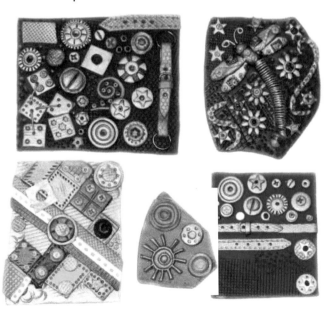

Making a zip:

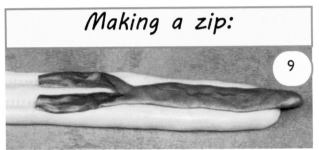

There are several ways to make a zip. I bought a silicone mould making kit, and made a mould using a metal zip (shown above). You can also buy a ready made zip mould, or press the clay into a zip to make the teeth, then sculpture the other parts. If you're using a mould, press some metalic clay into the mould, making sure it's not too thick.

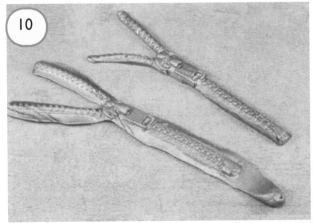

Once you've taken the clay out of the mould, trim the edges, as shown in the zip on the right. Don't worry that the zip is too large at the moment, we will cut it down later.

Place the zip as shown. As you can see, it is too long at the moment.

Cut two pieces of strap, and make a pointed end on one. Taking some wire, cut a piece and bend it to a U shape, with the middle part the same width as your strap. Cut another small piece, around 1cm long.

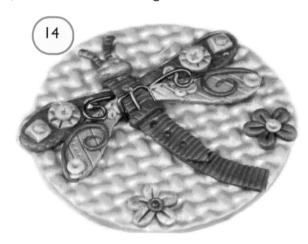

I cut the end of the zip off, shortened the zip, and replaced the end, it gives a nicer finish. I've also shortened the two split pieces, they will be the antenae.

Making a buckled strap:

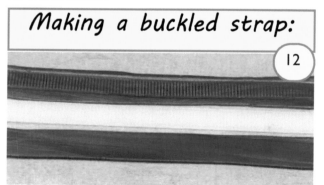

I use a plastic strap that has ridges on (shown in the middle of the two pieces of brown clay) to make the texture of the strap, but you can use anything, or even leave it un-textured.

Place the longer strap on first, then place the strap with the pointed end on top. Put the bent piece of wire in as shown, and push the small straight piece in to make the buckle prong. Cut a narrow piece of clay and place underneath the buckle. Finally, use a small ball tool and make equally spaced 'holes'. I finished this dragonfly off by making a silver head, antennae of thin straps, and some decorative flowers using 5mm teardrop cutters.

I've also added some wire that I curled round and pushed one end underneath the strap.

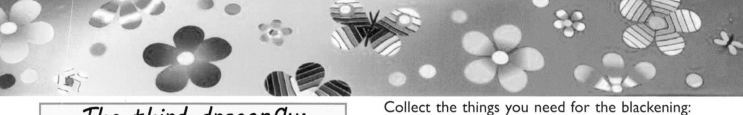

The third dragonfly:

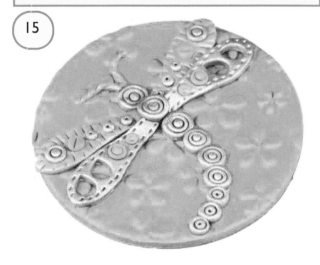

15

The final dragonfly body was made by rolling clay on PM5 and cutting circles, I cut 3 x 6mm, 3 x 5mm and 3 x 4mm diameter circles, then used smaller circle cutters to make circular marks on each circle. Start with the larger ones, and get smaller as you work towards the tail. I've made the antennae by twisting some copper clay.

Your pendants are now ready to cure. Put them on the same bowl you used to cure the backs on, make sure you press gently around the edges, and cure for an hour at the clay manufacturers recommended temperature.

Blackening the pendants:

16

Collect the things you need for the blackening: black acrylic paint (cheap is fine), a brush, some wet wipes, kitchen towel, cotton buds and a piece of foil.

17

Start by brushing the paint into half the pendant; it's best to do half at a time as you want to rub it off before it dries. Make sure you brush well into all the little nooks and crannies.

18

First take the kitchen towel and rub off the black paint, then use the cotton buds to get into the corners.

Then repeat up to this stage on the other side.

This is what it will look like when it's had both sides blackened.

19

Take the wet wipe and continue to rub off the black. You want to end up with black still in the crevices and textures, but not so much on the raised parts. Leave to dry completely before putting on the gilder paste.

The pendant on the left has been blackened, the one on the right before blackening. As you can see, the blackening gives the whole pendant depth, and when you add the metallic paste it really 'pops'.

Highlighting with metallic paste:

There are several different types of metallic paste, I use gilder paste by Pebeo and Inka Gold by Viva.

20

The pendant on the left has been blackened only, the one on the right has had the metallic paste added. To add the paste, put a very small amount on your finger and lightly rub it over the raised parts. It might be a good idea to either practice this, or do the back first. If you put on too much it can be wiped off with a wet wipe.

Start by highlighting the background, then work upwards. You will probably get some of the background paste on the dragonfly, but either wipe it off, or just go over it with the right coloured paste.

Once you've done the back and the front, leave it for a while to totally dry before the final part.

Putting it together:

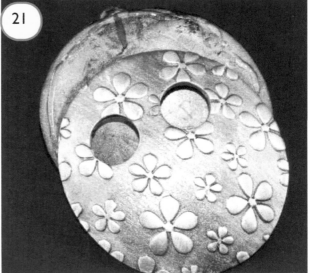

Before putting the two halves together you need to make a flat surface to join them. To do this take some 80 or 100 grit wet and dry sandpaper, wet both the sandpaper and the pendant part, then place the sandpaper on a flat surface wth the pendant half on top, design uppermost.

Using circular motions, gently rub the pendant half on the sandpaper until you have a flat surface all the way round the edge. Repeat with all pieces.

Take some superglue gel - I prefer using gel as it doesn't run everywhere - and put a line of glue all the way round the flat edge of the pendant front. Next take the back and line up the holes so the mark you made is in the middle of the two holes. Press gently together, turning it over to look at the pendant from the front to make sure non of the back is showing.

You now need to work out which way you want the pendant to sit, which way the dragonfly is facing. Once you've worked this out, make a mark on the underside of the top piece where you want the top of the pendant to be.

Think about how it's going to look once hung.

The finished pendants.
I like to give them a coat of varnish, I use Darwi Vernis. Although they don't need to be any shinier, I just feel that if they get wet the black paint won't run.

You can use satin varnish if you don't want the very shiny gloss look, or some wax.

109

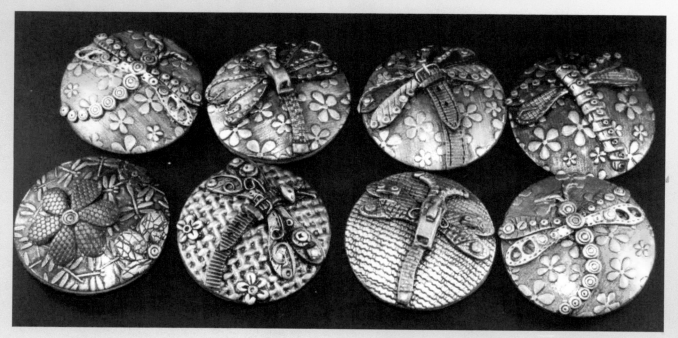

GALLERY:

This technique can be used on a variety of other projects. On the right is a mini jam jar covered with steampunk flowers and leaves, with a dragonfly on the lid.

Ammonite Snail:

I wanted to make something that was decorative but could have a practical use. So these snails can be used as ring holders while you do the washing up, and the shell cane can be made into a pendant.

TOOLS & MATERIALS:

- Pasta machine
- Tissue blade
- Craft knife
- Ruler
- Oven to cure clay in
- Tile to work on
- Small tile approximately 10cm x 10cm to cure your snail on
- Acrylic or metal clay roller
- Needle tool / cocktail stick
- Deli wrap for burnishing
- Circle cutter 4cm
- Circle cutters 4mm & 3mm for the eyes – not essential
- Tin foil 30cm x 30cm
- 24cm x 1mm wire. I buy it from the garden centre
- Pair of pliers, two pairs is ideal but one pair sufficient
- Cornflour – about a tablespoon is enough
- Metal bowl to cure pendants on – or any ceramic or metal curved surface if you are making a pendant
- Holographic embossing powder – optional
- Cyanoacrylate glue – commonly known as superglue

CLAY:

The clay for the snail above is as below. However, you can use any colours you like, whatever you have available as you don't need large amounts of each colour, just remember to use the same ratios in the blend, and keep the white parts in. I've used 56g packets of Premo clay throughout

- 1 x white
- 1 x cadmium yellow
- 1/2 x bronze
- 1/4 x raw sienna
- 1/4 x peacock pearl
- 1/4 x purple
- 1/4 x wasabi
- 1/4 x 18k gold
- 1/4 x silver
- 1/4 x copper
- 1/8 x wisteria
- 1/8 x alazarin crimson
- Scrap clay, around 10g

POLISHING MATERIALS:

If you want to varnish the pendant you will need polymer clay varnish. I use Darwi Vernis.

However, I like to sand and polish my snails, and this is what I use.
- 600 and 1000 grit wet and dry sandpaper
- Set of 6 micromesh sheets in 1500, 1800, 2400, 3600, 6000 & 12000 grit. I bought mine from Clayaround
- Rennaisance wax

Working out your blend:

I love playing with blends! However, it can use up a lot of clay, so I use a small circle cutter, around 1cm diameter and cut out circles of clay, roll them into logs, and see how they work together in blends.

I think the blend on the right is too dark, and the one on the left better, but needs a bit of tweaking.

To see how they're going to look in a cane, roll them up. I've put the lighter colour in the middle as that's the end thats going to be in the middle of the shell, so will be a smaller diameter.

The first two blends, going from the left, are the ones shown in the previous photo, the third one I liked but it needed more definition; the forth one I was happy with, so that's what I'm making the snail shell with.

Preparing the wire:

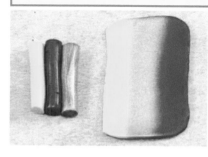

Choose three colours for the snail antennae, I've used purple, silver and wasabi.

Roll small logs of each, approx 5mm x 2.5cm, then make into a small Skinner blend. Put through pasta machine on PM1 & PM3. You want the blend to be 3cm wide, ie purple to wasabi as that's the length of each antennae.

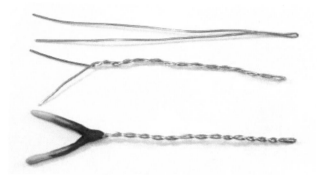

Take a 24cm piece of 1mm wire and fold in half. Using the pliers, twist from the folded end leaving 3cm untwisted, these will be the antennae.

Using your blend, cover the two 3cm pieces of wire, joining the clay at the bottom, in this case the purple end.

When cutting the clay, cut it at an angle, leaving the cut edge very fine. This will make it easier to blend it in, especially as I have silver in my blend; metallic clays usually show a line where they are joined, and making the overlap as thin as possible reduces the chance of a noticable join.

Smooth the join then cure for 15 minutes.

Making the ammonite snail shell cane:

1

Roll the clay on PM0 and using a 4cm circle cutter, cut the following:
1/2 x wisteria
1/2 x alizarin crimson
1/2 x white
1 x purple
1/2 x white
1 x wisteria
1/2 x white
1/2 x peacock pearl
1/2 x white
1 x wasabi
1/2 x silver
1/2 x 18k gold
1/4 x white
1/4 x 18k gold

2

Roll each into a 8cm log as shown in the photo, flatten slightly with your roller, fold in half bottom to top and put through the pasta machine.. Repeat until you have a nice Skinner blend.

The finished blend.

3

An optional step is to add some holographic embossing powder to the blend, then mix it in by putting through the pasta machine a few more times. This gives the snail shell a shimmer, but it's totally optional.

4

You now want a rectangle shape rather than the square shape shown on the left. In this case, fold your blend bottom to top as if you were continuing to make a Skinner blend, but this time put the blend through the pasta machine the other way, ie with the fold along the left or right hand side. This will make the blend longer and narrower.

Don't worry if it ends up wider than your pasta machine, we have a plan to cope with that!!

5

Now to manipulate the clay so that the finished cane shows more than one colour as you cut it. Hold the middle of the clay at the top in your left hand, and with your right fingers and thumb bently pull the clay down. Do this all the way down the blend, then hold the middle of the clay with your right hand, and with your left fingers and thumb, gently pull the left side of the clay downwards.

This is what you're aiming for. Don't worry if you split the clay, just push it back together, it will be fine once in a cane. This is the beauty of making organic projects, nature is better because it's not perfect.

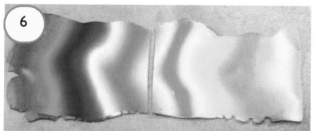

6

We now want to make the blend thinner, but as mentioned earlier the blend is going to be wider than your pasta machine. Just cut it in half and put each piece throught the pasta machine on PM2 then PM4. Then before rolling, just push the two pieces together and burnish (rub) well to adhere the join using deli paper and your finger.

7

From one of the long edges, roll the blend up. As you can see, due to the colour stripes being distorted, when you roll the cane up, there are no single blocks of colour in any part.

8

The clay that is going to cover the cane is made up of three colours.
<u>Colour 1:</u>   Bronze
<u>Colour 2:</u>   Off white. Add a little copper or brown to some white, approximately 7:1 ratio
<u>Colour 3:</u> You are looking for a honey coloured yellow. I rolled cadmium yellow, wisteria and raw sienna on PM0 and with a 2cm circle cutter, cut 7 1/4 yellow, 1/2 wisteria and 1/4 raw sienna. However, you can use any yellow/ocre colour you have, it's not imperative you do my blend.

Roll the three colours out on PM0 and cut a 5.5cm x 3.5cm rectangle of each colour. Sandwich them together with the off-white in the middle.

Pinch along both of the short (3.5cm) sides (this make it less likely that the clay will move when put through the pasta machine) and put through the pasta machine on PM0, PM2, PM4 and finally PM6.
This makes a long, thin blend.

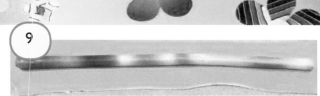

9

With the yellow colour inside and the bronze outside, cover the cane.

10

Once covered, roll the clay to 42cm, with the darker (purple) end measuring 15mm diameter and the lighter (gold) end measuring 5mm diameter.

11

You're now going to cut the cane into 21 x 2cm pieces (I haven't shown them all in the photo).

12

The next part is important. Turn each piece round, but make sure you turn them all the same way, eg left side of each to the front. This way you don't get two identical colours next to each other. You can really see the effect of manipulating the clay by the variated colours in each piece of cane.

13

Roll on PM0 some bronze clay and some more of colour 3 on step 8. Cut a rectangle of each, 2.5cm x 6cm, pinch one short end and put it through the pasta machine, short end down, on PM0. PM2 and PM4.

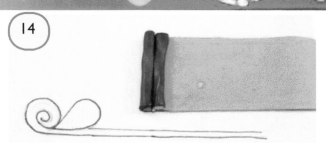

14

Curl up one end of the strip, dark side on the outside, for about one and a bit turns. Now take the smallest of your 2cm cane segments and make it into a teardrop shape. Place it on the yellow side of the bronze/honey strip, with the pointed end of the teardrop pushed into the bottom of the curl, resting on the honey side of the strip. The drawing under the photo shows where you are putting the first segment.

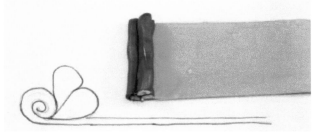

Take the second segment of cane, again make it into a teardrop shape, and place the pointed end in the gap between the first segment and the curl; as shown in the drawing above. Make sure you keep all the segments the same way as you laid them out earlier so that each segment looks different.

Continue making each segment into a teardrop, putting it next to the previous one, and wrap the strip round them as shown.

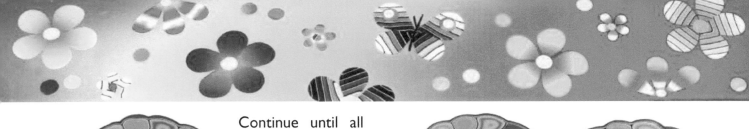

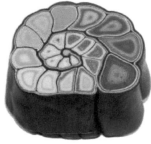

Continue until all the segments are in, then tuck the strip round the last one and cut off any excess.

Cut two slices from the cane, 3mm thick. You can see that the one on the left is on the scrap clay covered foil and is the same size.

Making the shell:

Take a piece of foil 30cm x 30cm, start by gently pushing it into a ball, then carefully pressing it into the same size and shape of the cane (as shown on the photo above on the right). To make the edges smooth, roll it on the work surface.

Put the two slices either side of the foil piece. As you can see, they dont meet in the middle, but the slices have been cut thick enough for them to be stretched to fit.

Once you're happy with the size and shape, you want to make the top and two sides into more of a point, rather than a flat surface. Do this by rolling the edges on the work surface. This is the view from the top.

Then cover with scrap clay rolled on PM4.

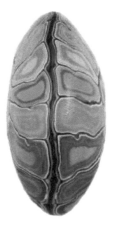

Gently pinch the two cane slices all the way round so that they meet. Try and match the two sides so each segment mirrors the one on the other side. This is a different coloured cane. Pinch all the way round, including the base.

You can see from this view the the bottom is flat but the top and sides have been made into a point.

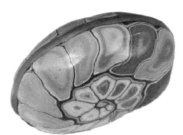

In this photo I've added a thin strip of clay which is cut from the snail body blend, and you can either do this, or leave it plain. Once you've finished the shell, burnish it well and make as smooth as possible, then cure for 1 hour.

116

Making the snail body:

To make the blend for the snail body, roll five colours of clay on PM0; I've used wasabi, peacock pearl, silver, wisteria and purple. Cut half a 4cm circle of each and roll into 5cm logs.

Make into a Skinner blend, then if you're going to put a strip round your snail shell, cut off a small piece from the end as shown. Lengthen the piece by putting it through the pasta machine on a smaller setting until it is the right length to go round the shell. Then put through the pasta machine on PM3 with the stripes going downwards so it doesn't get any wider. Cut a 3mm strip and wrap round the middle of the shell, where the two edges of the canes meet.

Roll some scrap clay on PM0 and cut a piece the length of the twisted wire, 1cm wide.
Bend the twisted wire 2cm below the end of the antennae.
Wrap the clay round the twisted wire.

The photo on the left is the scrap clay wrapped round, with the join on the top. the photo on the right shows the clay burnished so the join is smooth, the part near the antennae blended smoothly, and the tail made into a point.

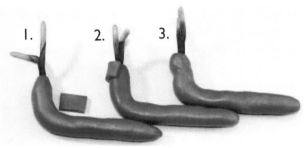

1. Add a second layer of scrap clay, 2.5cm wide and wrap round and burnish as before. Cut a small piece of clay 1.5cm x 1cm on PM0.
2. Place the small piece of clay on the face area
3. Blend in the small piece of clay, making a more pronounced head.

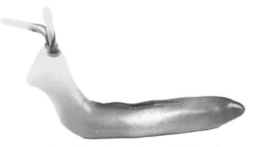

Lengthen the blend so the width is the same length as the snail body, then put through on PM4 at that width.

Cover the body as shown, with the join on top. Burnish the join well using deli paper and your finger.

I've made tiny logs of clay and wrapped them round the base of each antennae, just to give some extra colour and interest.

117

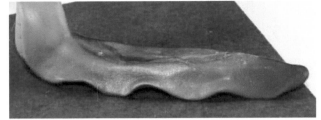

Before you put the eyes and nose on, you're going to make the front of the snail and the frilly sides.

Start to pinch under where the nose will go, then down either side , making a central front part. Continue to pinch all the way round both sides of the snail making a thinner edge and flatter base, as shown below. Once done, make horizontal lines all the way down the front part, then add the eyes and nose.

With your finger and thumb, pinch along the bottom edge making it even thinner, and then push up some parts, making it wavy.

Press the shell hard into the snail body, make sure the frilly sides are how you want them, then remove the shell and cure the body for 1 hour.

Finishing your snail:

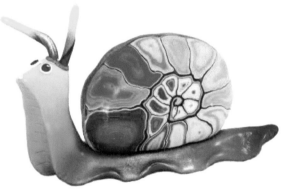

For the eyes roll some white clay on PM6 and cut out two 4mm circles. Roll a darker colour clay, I've used purple, on PM6 and cut two 3mm circles.

If you don't have these size circle cutters you can use flattened little balls of clay instead.

To make the highlight, put a tiny triangle of white in the top corner of each eye. The nose is a very small ball of any coloured clay.

Place your snail on a small tile and dust some cornflour on the part where the shell will go.

Either polish or varnish the two parts separately before glueing them together.

To get a lovely shine I use wet and dry sandpaper grit 600 then 1000, then 6 micromesh sheets, also wet, in 1500, 1800, 2400, 3600, 6000 and 12000. Finally I rub some renaissance wax into each part and buff. I have a dremel for this, but a piece of denim also works well.

Using some metallic and pearlescant clay in the blends gives a wonderful shine when polished.

118

Flying ducks:

I watched Coronation Street, an English soap opera, for 16 years, and a character called Hilda Ogden had a set of three flying ducks on her wall. They were the height of poor taste at the time, but have become collectors items. They're a bit 'love them or hate them', but I've always loved them, so this is my take on Hilda's ducks.

DECLAN. DONNA & DOUGLAS DUCKS:

This is the duck that I'll be teaching in this tutorial, and the amount of clay is for the one duck. I'll show you how I do the different techniques for the larger and smaller ducks but the amount of clay needed is around the same as for the middle duck - the one will be making.

TOOLS & MATERIALS:

- Pasta machine
- Tissue blade
- Craft knife • Ruler
- Oven to cure clay in
- Tile to work on
- Acrylic or metal clay roller
- Needle tool / cocktail stick
- Deli wrap
- Cardboard 14cm x 14cm
- Texture sheet. or sandpaper
- Soap stone for burnishing – or a smooth stone. bone folder or credit card can also be used
- Circle cutters 3mm. 5mm. 1cm (tube) and 3cm
- A pair of pliers
- 1mm wire – I get this from a garden centre. You need 15cm for each duck
- Gold mica powder – optional
- If you want to varnish the pendant you will need polymer clay varnish. I use Darwi Vernis

CLAY:

You can use any green. orange and purple clay for the duck. but to make the green and orange mixes I've used in the duck above you'll need the following. All clay is premo. in 56g blocks.
- Ultramarine – 1/4 block
- Zinc yellow – 1/2 block
- Fuschia – 1/4 block
- 18k gold – 1/2 block
- White – 1 block
- Black – 1/2 block
- Scrap clay – 56g. quivalent to 1 block
- Clay for back of duck – any colour. about 3/4 of a block

Orange: mix 1/4 block of ultramarine & 1/4 a block of zinc yellow.

Green: mix 1/4 block ultramarine & 1/4 blcok zinc yellow

119

Making the template:

There are loads of pictures of flying ducks on the Internet, I can't show you as they may be copyrighted, but here are a few of my drawings of the different shapes you could use.

You first need to decide what size duck you want to make, and whether it's going to have one or two wings. I've put a photo above to show you how each look. You also need to decide whether your duck is having a closed or open beak; duck on the left has a closed one, the duck on the right has an open beak. Draw your duck on cardboard, and cut it out; you need two ducks. Cut off the beak and the leg, but before cutting the leg off make a pencil mark of where it was, and the angle. This is so you know where to put the leg back! The template below is the size I made my duck.

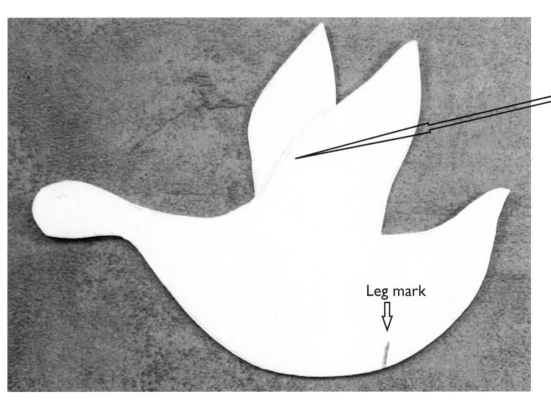

Draw a line showing where the front wing is.

You'll need the second cardboad template so you have a pattern of the wing for adding an extra layer of clay at a later time.

Leg mark

Making the beak and foot:

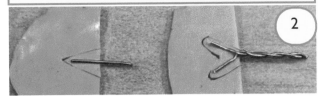

If you're going to make a closed beak, cut a 2cm piece of wire, lay it on PM2 18k gold, or any yellow colour clay and cut a triangular beak shape. If you're making an open beak, cut a 6cm piece of wire, fold it in half and twist from the folded end, leaving 1cm untwisted. Bend apart the two ends as shown and put on PM2 clay, cutting an open beak shape.

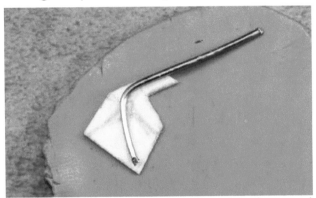

For the foot, cut a piece of wire 6cm long and bend it at a right angle at 1cm from the end. Take the cardboard leg template and lay on the same colour clay you used for the beak. Lay the wire on to make sure it's the right shape and cut round the template, then remove it.

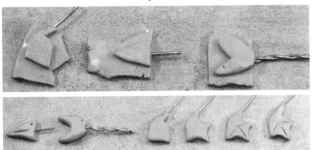

Lay the pieces on more PM2 clay and cut round them, incasing the wire between the clay. Pinch all round the edges of the beak and foot to lose the gap between the two pieces of clay, and smooth the edges.

For the straight beak make a light line from the tip of the beak to 3/4 of the way along. For both beaks put a small hole in the top to denote the nostril.

For the feet, once you've pinched all the way round and smoothed the join, make the feet more web-like by pushing in between the points in three places. Make three lines from the middle of the foot to the three points, I've then used gold mica powder to make the beak and foot really shiny, but this is optional.

Once done, cure the beak and foot for 30 minutes at the clay manufacturers recommended temperature. I use Premo and cure at 130° C.

Covering the template in scrap clay:

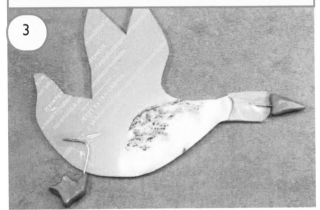

Before covering the scrap clay, tape the beak and foot to the UNDERSIDE of the cardboard template. I didn't do this when making the duck and found that you can see the wire through the head and body clay. Also, bend the end of the foot wire as shown, otherwise it will come out, and you'll have to superglue it back in again - I learned that the hard way!!!

You can really see the shape of the wire on my duck head.

It's a case of do what I say, not what I did!

4

Roll scrap clay on PM2, lay the duck on and cut round, then lay it on the other side and cut round. Pinch the clay all the way round to join and make a smooth edge.

Work out at what angle you want your duck to by flying and using a needle tool, make two holes 1cm apart at the base of the wing. As you can see the holes are horizontal so my duck will fly as shown. Cure 1 hour.
While it's curing, start making the feather cane 1 up to step 17, this will give it time to rest and firm up before cutting.

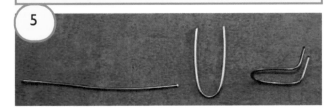

Adding the back and hanging wire:

5

Cut a piece of wire 6cm, fold in half and bend the two ends up 1.5cm from the end.
The angle you bend the wire up should be slightly less than 90 degrees.

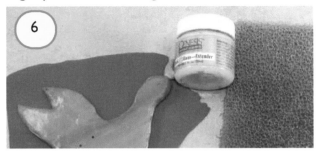

6

As you're adding raw clay to cured clay you need to use some polymer clay adhesive to bond the two. I use Genesis, but any clay adhesive will work. Roll some clay of the colour you're going to back the duck with, on PM4. I like to texture the backing clay by using a sponge as shown.

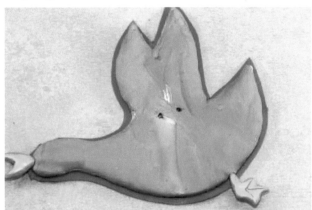

Cover the underside of the duck, and the edges with the clay adhesive, then lay the duck on the clay and cut 5mm wider than the duck all round. Fold the extra clay over the edges.

7

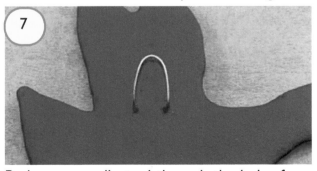

Push your needle tool through the holes from the other side, then push the two ends of wire through the two holes.

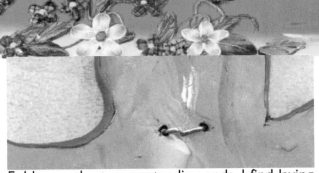

Fold over the two protruding ends, I find laying the duck on the work surface and pushing the ends down with the pliers the easiest way to do this. Make sure the edges of the backing clay are smooth all the way round. Cure 30 minutes with the backing side uppermost.

Covering the head, body and far wing:

8

Roll some 18k gold and green clay on PM0 and cut a 3cm circle of each. Roll into a log, flatten with your roller, fold in half offset a little and put through the pasta machine. Keep folding and putting through the pasta machine until you have a blend.

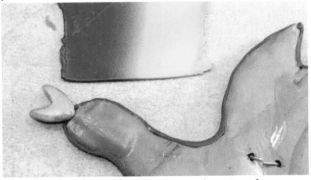

Make sure your clay is the right size for your duck's head, and roll to PM3. Put some polymer clay adhesive on the head and edges, lay the duck's head on the gold/green blend.

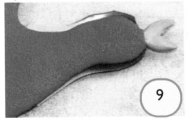

9

Cut around 5mm wider than the head and carefully smooth the clay over the head and edges.

10

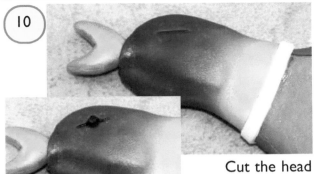

Cut the head blend at an angle where the collar is going to be. Cut a thin strip of white on PM3 and butt next to the head as shown. Then with some deli wrap or plain white paper and a burnishing tool, gently burnish the head to remove any finger marks. For the eye, make a small line with your needle tool and insert a very thin log of clay. Make an indentation with a ball tool and put in a small black ball of clay for the eye.

If you'd like your duck's eye to stand out more, roll a ball of a lighter colour clay first, insert ther press with the ball tool and then add a smaller ball of black.

11

Now take your second cardboard duck template, draw where the wing will go; as you can see by the thick black line I've drawn, it goes slightly lower than the body line. #cut out the right wing. If you're making a single wing duck you still need to do this as it covers the hanging wire.

Roll some scrap clay on PM0 and cut out the wing shape.

Put polymer clay adhesive on the wing area and add the wing. Smooth the edges by pushing them down gently with your finger all the way round.

123

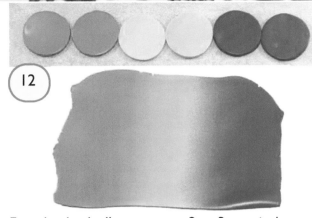

12

For the body I've cut out 2 x 3cm circles on PM0 of orange, 18k gold and purple. Roll each colour into a log and make a blend as you did in step 8.

Get your blend to the width of the duck body, then roll to PM3.
Cover the duck as you did for the head, don't worry about how much of the wing you cover, most of it will be covered by wing feathers.
Finally, make sure all the edges are smooth and burnish the whole body.

13

14

For the blend covering the back wing, cut a half 3cm circle of orange, 18k gold and purple on PM0 and make into a blend, again on PM3.

Cover the back wing and make marks on the front wing of where you want each set of feathers to go; this makes it easier to place them.

15

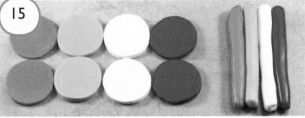

On PM0 cut out 2 x 3cm circles in orange, 18k gold, white and purple, roll into 7cm logs and make a blend as you did in step 8.

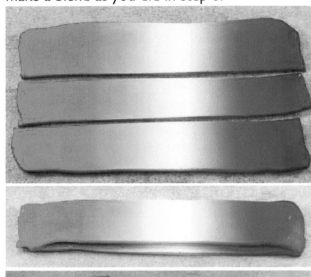

Cut the blend in three and stack. Pinch both short ends then put through the pasta machine on PM0, PM2, PM4 & PM6, short end first, making a long thin blend.

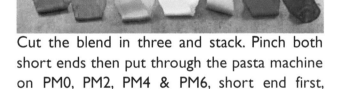

16

Fold the clay backwards and forwards, making a 2cm plug - photo on left.

124

Then, squish your nicely made plug in various directions. Push your thumb into it, and pull it back into shape. This is a really important step and makes the lovely watercolour effect on the feather. The photo on the right shows the plug after being squished about.

Make the plug into a rectangle measuring 5cm long and 2cm wide.
With the back of your blade, make around 14 marks on the diagonal as shown. These are where you are going to cut. Notice how lovely the blend has become with the colours in waves since you squished it.

Cut the cane in half and turn one side round, making the veins in a V shape. Put the two halves together lightly, don't press them together, you just need them together so you can take a 1cm circle cutter and make a mark in the middle at the top, around 1cm from the top. After you've made the mark, separate the two halves and, using the circle cutter, cut down the two half circles.

Roll some white clay on PM0 and cut a rectangle 10cm long by the height of your cane. Put it on PM0 black and cut round.

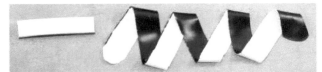

Pinch the two short ends (this stops the clay separating into a Y shape when you put it through the pasta machine), and put it through, short end downwards, on PM0, PM2, PM4 & PM6, giving you a long thin piece of black/white clay which is going to make the feather veins.

Cut 3cm circles on PM0 of white, 18k gold and green, roll into logs and make a blend, as shown on step 8, then fold in half and put through the pasta machine, short end first, on PM0, PM2, PM4 & PM6.

Cut where the top line is and lay the piece of cane on the black/white blend. Cut to size and replace. Repeat with the next cut until all are covered. Make sure you always put the piece you cut off onto the blend, this way the black/white will be the same way up on all cuts.

Roll up, white end first, then when you get to the gold part, roll back and forward, leaving a gap of white at the bottom, and when you get to the green part, go round the whole cane once or twice. This isn't imperative, I just prefer it as I like more white at the base but a normal bullseye cane will work well too.

125

Roll some purple clay on PM6, cut the cane in half and cover one side 3/4 of the way up. Put the two halves together. Finally cover the cane with some black/white clay on PM6 (the same as you used to make the veins). This part isn't shown on the photo!

21

For the centre vein, follow instructions in step 20 up to making the long thin strip, but instead of making a rolled cane, make a plug by fan folding the clay 1cm wide.

Use your roller to flatten the stack, keeping the width the same, until you can put it through the pasta machine on PM0, short end first. Fold in half with the white inside and put through on PM0 again. This will make the centre vein.

22

Roll the circular cane to 1cm diameter and cut a piece to fit the round hole. Put a strip of the second blend in between the two half canes.

For covering the cane roll some white, black and 18k gold on PM0. Cut 4 cm by the width of the cane.

Stack the colours, black inside, and put through the pasta machine, short end first, on PM0, PM2 & PM4, then cover the cane, gold on the outside.

To make it look more like a feather, round the top and bottom and make the bottom slightly narrower.

Making feather 2:

23

This cane is made from two coloured canes; one orange and one green. For the orange cane cut 1/2 black, 2 x orange and 2 white 3cm circles on PM0. For the green cane replace orange for green. Make each into blends following the technique on step 8.

24

Make each blend into a plug by folding the blend in half, putting through the pasta machine short end first on PM0, PM2, PM4 & PM6 then fan folding to a plug. Cut off around 9cm of the dark end as it would be too dark if you use it all, but a little bit really gives the cane depth. Make the plug 4cm long by 1cm high.

126

25

You should have enough black/white strip from feather 1 to make the veins, but if you don't make some more by cutting black and white clay on PM0, 4cm x 1cm. Make 11 marks in each plug then make them into veins the same way as feather 1.

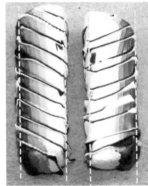

Place the canes as shown, so the veins make a V shape and the white is on the inside. I suggest you carefully trim the outside and inside edges so that any overhanging pieces of black/white strip

don't look messy in the finished cane. I've put little cut lines in yellow on the photo to show where I mean. Only cut a very very small slither off. I didn't do this and the cane still worked out well so it's an optional step.

26

For the central vein cut 1/2 black, 2 x purple and 2 x white 3cm circles on PM0. Follow step 8 to make a blend.

Fold the blend in half and put through the pasta machine, thin end first, on PM0, PM2, PM4 & PM6. Make a plug 1.5cm wide, then with your clay roller roll to 6cm long, before putting it though the pasta machine on PM0.

Cut a 5cm piece off, fold in half with the white inside, and put though the pasta machine again on PM0. This is your central vein, insert it between the orange and green canes.

Roll the remaining piece of clay on PM2 & PM4 and cover the cane as shown.

It's now ready to reduce and use.

Adding the feathers:

Before adding the feathers, cover the edge of the front wing on the right side with some of the backing colour. This is so any gaps in the end of the feathers won't show scrap clay.

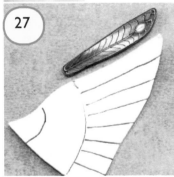

27

Take your cardboard wing template and reduce feather 1 to the right length and width. Make sure it isn't wider in the middle or the slices won't fit nicely.

Cut the cane in half, and before cutting a slice, press the cane on the work surface or tile and press down the top end, forming an angle. Work out which side of the cane you want on the top and put that edge on the tile. In the photo above the side of the cane with orange at the top will have been on the work surface.

Cut three slices of cane, around 2-3mm thick. Start placing the feathers on the wing. You can see now why we covered the edge of the wing with purple as you can just see it between the first two feathers. Notice the angle of the top of the feathers, make sure the point of each feather is uppermost.

I also use this cane for the tail feathers. Make the bottom end of the cane pointed and cut three x 3mm slices. Press them on the tail end.

As you go down the wing, slightly reduce the size of the feather cane to make them fit better.
Continue until you have the whole of the first layer filled. You should be able to get all feathers for the wing from half the cane, leaving the other half for another duck. However, if needed you can use the other half cane, so don't worry if you make any mistakes, there is plenty of cane.

(29)

For the last feathers, the ones closest to the neck, use the same cane as you made for the circle at the top of the first feather cane. Lay 1mm slices on as shown. Finally make some light lines on the back wing to look like feathers.

Making the flower decorations:

(30)

Cut 3cm circles of purple, 18k gold, green and white on PM0. Make into a blend as in step 8, fold the blend in half, pinch the short ends and make a long thin blend up to PM6 as shown in step 18.

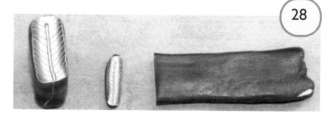

(28)

Reduce cane 2 to the size of the second layer of feathers. Make sure the top end is rounded and cut 2mm slices. Add to the wing as shown in the next photo.

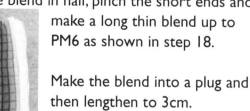

Make the blend into a plug and then lengthen to 3cm.

Make around 11 cuts, 2mm apart

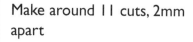

Take each slice and off-set it by around 2mm as shown.

Once all are off-set, trim off the excess white and purple parts and push the cane into a circle.

Cover with black/white strip on PM6.

Lengthen the cane until it measures 4mm diameter, then pinch the purple side to make a teardrop shape; cut 1mm slices and arrange in flower patterns on the duck body. For the flower centres roll 18k gold on PM5, cover with mica powder and cut 3mm circles.

Cure your duck for 30 minutes, then once cool you can leave it as it is or varnish it with polymer clay varnish.

Making the larger and smaller ducks:

If you want to make a larger duck, lay your template on cardboard and cut around 5mm larger all the way round. For the smaller duck cut a template 5mm smaller all round.

These are the templates I made. In hindsight I should have made the smaller one's neck a little shorter and the larger one's neck a little longer.

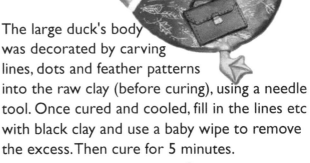

The large duck's body was decorated by carving lines, dots and feather patterns into the raw clay (before curing), using a needle tool. Once cured and cooled, fill in the lines etc with black clay and use a baby wipe to remove the excess. Then cure for 5 minutes.

To decorate the small duck's body I've used a silkscreen and white acrylic paint. Do this on the blend before you put it on the body and let it dry fully before adding.

This duck was made with peacock pearl, wasabi, purple and 18k gold.

Linda Hyam made this lovely duck using Premo green, cadmium red, purple & 18k gold.

These three ducks were made using the patterns shown as examples of templates on the second page.

This duck used a plum colour made by mixing 1/4 packet of alazarin crimson with 1/8 packet each of cobalt blue & white. The other colours were wasabi, the green I made for the tutorial duck, and 18k gold.

For this duck I used alcohol ink on the body and head instead of blends.

This duck says that unlike most ducks, she doesn't like rain! Her body is decorated using mica powder and a stencil from Clayaround.

Instead of flowers, I've used slices of cane used in the feather one, and also as the third wing feather.

The stencil is a lotus flower, turned upside down, and adding some handles.

Petoskey Stone:

TOOLS & MATERIALS:

FOR THE CANE:
- Pasta machine
- Tissue blade
- Ruler
- Oven to cure clay in
- Tile to work on
- Acrylic or metal clay roller

FOR THE PENDANT:
- White paper to make templates
- Needle tool / cocktail stick. circle cutters. ruler – for textures – optional
- Texture sponge. or sandpaper
- Circle cutter 7cm – optional
- Cornflour
- Metal bowl to cure pendants on – or any ceramic or metal curved surface
- Polymer clay adhesive. eg Bake & Bond. Genesis. Polyclay etc
- 80 & 600 grit wet and dry sandpaper
- 6mm knitting needle for bail
- Wire choker
- Superglue
- If you want to polish your pendant. I use 600 and 1000 grit wet and dry sandpaper. then micromesh sheets in 1500. 1800. 2400. 3600. 6000 & 12000
- If you want to varnish any part of the pendant you will need polymer clay varnish. I use Darwi Vernis

Petoskey Stone consists of tightly packed, six-sided corallites, which are the skeletons of the once-living cor-al polyps. The dark center (or eyes) were the mouth of the coral. The lines surrounding the eyes were once tentacles which brought food into the mouth. The Petoskey Stone, like the city, was named for the Ottawa Chief Pe-to-se-ga (Rising Sun) because the stones pattern looks like the rays of the sun. It is only found in Michigan, and is their state stone.

The Petoskey stone is predominently shades of grey, but there are some rare pink stones, which is the reason I made a red/pink coloured cane as well as the grey one.

DR RON LEHOCKY:

Dr Ron Lehcoky has created thousands of polymer clay heart pins and sold them for $10 each in aid of the Kids Centre for Pediatric Therapies in Kentucky. He's a huge hero for me, so imagine how I felt when he commented on my Petosky stone pendants. I sent him some of each of the canes and he made some of his wonderful hearts with them.

A real petoskey stone:

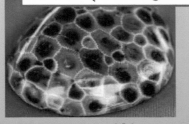

CLAY:

For the pink cane:
- Premo Pearl
- Premo Gold
- Premo Bronze
- Premo Alizarin
- Premo Transulcent
- Premo White

For the black/white/grey cane:
- Premo Black
- Premo White
- Premo Pearl

Preparing the seven different blends:

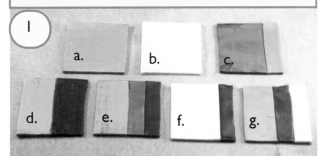

Roll the clay out on the thickest setting of your pasta machine, PM0 and cut a 5cm x 5cm (2" x 2") square of the following colours:

a. Gold
b. Pearl
c. 3/4 Bronze, 1/4 Gold
d. 1/2 Gold, 1/2 Alizarin
e. 1/2 Gold, 1/4 Bronze, 1/4 Alizarin
f. 3/4 Pearl, 1/4 Alizarin
g. 1/2 Gold, 1/4 Alizarin, 1/4 Pearl

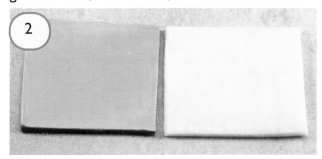

Roll out translucent also to PM0 and cut 7 squares, 5cm x 5cm. Put one square of translucent clay with each of the coloured squares.

Mix each square with a translucent square, making 7 different blends.

With your blade, chop each of the blends up separately. You want to chop them up so the pieces are quite small.

On a large tile, make a square of the different blends, one end (the bottom in the picture) being the darkest, and gradually getting lighter to the other end. Try to mix the colours up a bit, you don't want a uniform blend from dark to light. Once you're happy with your blend,

use your roller to adhere all the clay and make it into a slab.

7

Cut your slab into four equal squares.

8

Take a square and roll it through the pasta machine on PM0, PM2, PM4 and finally PM6. Make sure you put it through from the darkest end to the lightest, and keep putting it through each time the same way.

9

Roll it into a log, darker end first, ending with the lighter end on the outside.
Repeat steps 8 & 9 with the other three squares, you'll now have four logs. Next, squash each log to 1cm high. Do this by firstly rolling the log 'inwards' to make it shorter and fatter, then I use the pad of my thumb to do the final 'squashing'.

10

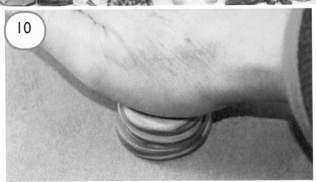

11

Do this for all four logs, then stack them, and squash the stack to 3.5cm high.

Making the lines:

12

Cut the stack in half, and on each half mark around 13 lines, radiating from the centre as shown.

13

Roll some Pearl and white clay on PM0, cut:
15cm x 5.5cm (6" x 2") in pearl clay
5.5cm x 5.5cm (2" x 2") in white clay
Mix the two strips together to make a pearly-white colour, then roll out, starting with PM0, then getting thinner and thinner until it's at PM8. Cut one of the triangular segments off the half stack. Cut a strip of the pearly-white clay the same width as the height of the stack and lay the triangular segment on it.

Cover the triangular segment around 2/3rds to 3/4 down each side towards the point. The petoskey stone is organic, so the lines need to be irregular; make sure you vary the length from segment to segment.

Continue cutting a slice, covering with the pearly-white strip, and placing it next to the previously covered one.

NOTE:

It is really important that you put each segment back the same way, so keep checking as you go along, looking at each side and making sure it is the right way up.

You can see in the picture to the left the part that's been covered, and I've turned the remaining piece up the other way so you can see clearly that the pattern is different.

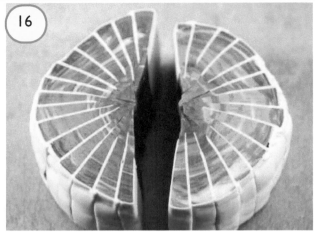

Finish covering all the segments on each half, then put the two halves together.

Reducing the cane:

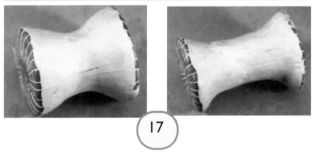

Start reducing the cane by squeezing gently in the middle until it is around 3.5cm diameter, then pushing from the middle out towards each end. This is how I reduce canes, but if you have a preferred method, that's fine.

Once it's 30cm long, cut off the distorted ends and cut into four equal pieces.

18

You're going to make a variety of canes of differing diameters. To do this roll each of the four pieces to 12mm diameter and cut a 2.5cm (1") piece off each end (8 pieces) - put them to one.

Roll the remaining four canes to 10mm diameter and cut some 2.5cm pieces off. You need a variety of 12mm, 10mm, 8mm and 5mm diameter canes for the petoskey stone cane. See the previous photo for the ones I made. If you don't have enough cane for the smaller ones, reduce one or two of the 12mm ones.

Assembling the cane:

19

Now for the fun part, assembling the cane. I like to make it in a rectangular shape as it's easier to use in projects. Make sure you get a nice mix of sizes and shades of colour.

20

Once you're happy with it, gently push it into a rectangular cane.

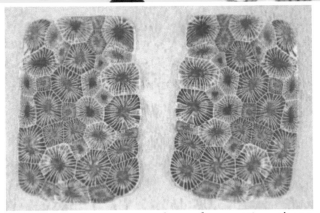

I used my Lucy cane slicer for cutting these slices so I could get as many slices as possible out of the cane. I recommend that you rest the cane in the fridge for an hour or so before slicing, whether using a slicer or by hand. You can really see the different colours of the canes in this photo, and I could have paid more attention to the colours as there are some similar ones together. But hey, it's organic. I love that word, it covers a lot of mistakes!

Making a black, white and grey cane:

For this cane we're just using black and white for the canes, and pearl and white for the lines. Again, we're making 5cm x 5cm squares on PM0, and putting equal amounts of translucent with each.

- 7/8 white, 1/8 black
- 1/2 white, 1/2 black
- 1/8 white, 7/8 black
- 3/4 white, 1/4 black
- 1/4 white, 3/4 black
- 1/2 black only

135

This time, instead of making one large rectangle and cutting it into four, I made four separate smaller rectangles. As before, make them go from dark to light as shown.

Then follow steps 8 - 19 in the rose coloured cane, still using the pearl/white mixture to make the lines.

For this cane I've cut the canes slightly longer, around 4cm long, but still made the varying size diameters.

Before you press the cane too closely together,

cut it in half (the reason we made slightly longer canes) then put the two pieces together. This makes a larger cane.

The finished cane.

Making the pendants:

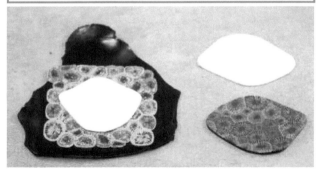

Cut a stone shape in paper and cut out. Roll out some black clay on PM3, lay the Petoskey stone cane on it and smooth with your roller to combine the two, making sure there are no air bubbles Place the paper template on and cut round.

NOTE: You can use any shape you like for these pendants, including cutters you may already have. I just like the more organic look, as the cane is of a stone, so draw loads of freehand four sided shapes on a large piece of paper until I find one I like.

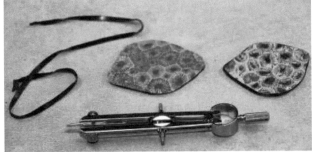

As these parts are going to be placed on a backing before curing, I like to edge them in black for a more professional and neat appearance. To do this you need a thin strip of black, the width of the edge of the pendant. I use a double needle compass to make this really easy, but a ruler and scalpel also work. Roll out black clay on PM7, cut the strip and attach it all round the edge of the pendant.

Making a texture sheet:

You can use a commercial texture sheet, or if you prefer, make your own.

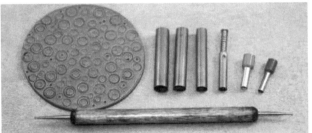

Roll out some scrap clay on PM0 and lightly mark out a 7cm circle (this is so you know how much of the clay you need to texture). With a variety of circle cutters, make indentations in the clay as shown. When happy with it, cut out the 7cm circle and cure in the oven at the clay manufacturers recommended time for 1 hour.

Two others, one with dots, one with lines.

Adding the texture:

Roll out some black clay on PM3. Dust cornflour onto the clay, and using your roller, roll the black clay firmly over the texture piece.

Lay the stone pendant piece lightly on the black textured clay and cut the desired shape out of the black clay. Don't worry about the cornflour, that will wash off once cured.

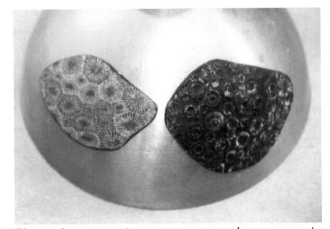

Place the two pieces on a metal or ceramic bowl - I get my 12cm diameter metal bowl from Ikea.

Making a bail:

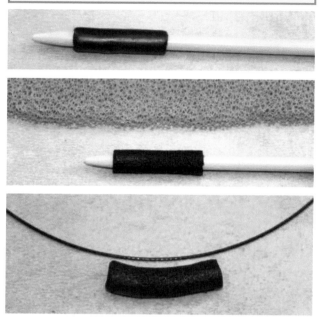

Backing the pendant:

Roll out some black clay on PM3 and texture with the same texture as you used on the bail. Put some clay adhesive on the back of the pendant and add the textured clay. Smooth down (using the texture to prevent fingermarks) and trim. Finally put some clay adhesive on the bail and push that firmly onto the textured clay.

I like to cure this in a tin with cornflour in it so that the shape can be supported. Cure with the bail side uppermost for 30 minutes.

Roll out some black clay on PM3 and wrap round a 6mm diameter knitting needle. Put some cornflour on the needle first to prevent the clay sticking. Make the length of the bail around 3-4cm, but it really depends on the size of your pendant.

Using a texture sheet, sandpaper or sponge, texture the bail, then remove it from the needle.

Take your choker wire and carefully bend the bail to the same curved shape as the wire.

Finally, place on the bowl with the pendant parts and cure all the pieces for 1 hour.

Using gilder paste, put a very small amount on your finger and lightly brush it across the texture as shown. Go really carefully with this, it is far better to not put enough on than put too much on as one on, it cant be removed easily. You're only putting it on the parts that will show round the edge so don't need to to do the whole thing. If you really aren't happy with it, you can take the whole lot off with some baby wipes and start again.

I used gilding wax from Pebeo, but also have used Inca Gold from Viva, I buy both from Clayaround but they're sold on various sites.

Finishing your pendant:

Before putting the two pieces together, I like to polish the stone part. This is optional, you can varnish it if you prefer but I like the softer, more natural look for this cane. To do this I used wet and dry sandpaper first in 600grit then 1000grit. I then use the Micromesh sheets which go from 1500 to 12000 grit. Finally I put Renaissance wax on it, let it dry, then buff with a dremel, but rubbing with denim or a towel also brings it up well.
I then varnish the back piece with clay varnish - I use Darwi Vernis.

A stone made from the cane, with slices of the individual canes, showing the difference in colour between them.

Finally, using superglue, glue the two peices together, and your pendant is finished.

Dr Ron Lehocky's wonderful hearts using the petoskey stone canes.

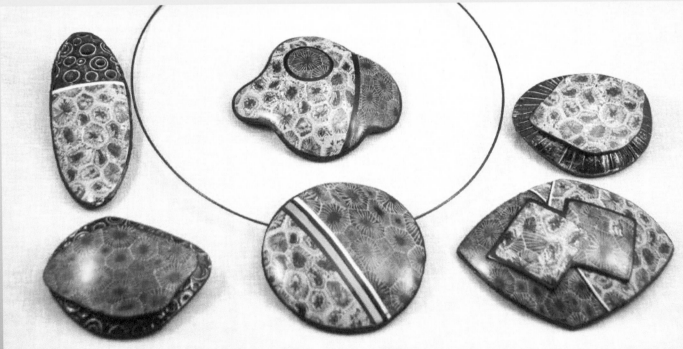

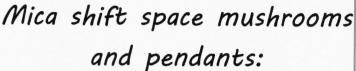

Mica shift space mushrooms and pendants:

TOOLS & MATERIALS:

I love metallic clay and use both Cernit and Premo in the same blend. I cure them at 130°C for an hour.

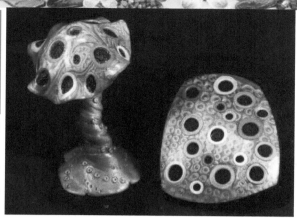

- Pasta machine
- Tissue blade – flexible
- Craft knife • Ruler
- Oven to cure clay in
- Tile to work on
- Acrylic or metal clay roller
- Needle tool / cocktail stick
- Deli wrap
- Texture sheet, sponge or sandpaper
- Soap stone for burnishing – or a smooth stone, bone folder or credit card can also be used
- Circle cutters in various sizes. I use 11mm, 9mm, 8mm, 7mm, 6mm and 4mm. Some of these are Kemper cutters, others I bought from the Internet, and others are Ferrule bootlace crimps, used by electricians, but very cheap to buy
- 1mm and 2mm ball tools
- Metal bowl to cure pendants on – or any ceramic or metal curved surface
- 600 grit wet and dry sandpaper
- Polymer clay adhesive – I use either Kato polypaste or Genesis thick medium extender

ADDITIONAL TOOLS:

Additional tools needed for the mushrooms:
- 6cm circle cutter – although you could cut out a 6cm circle in card and cut round this instead
- A small light bulb, the one I use is 4.5cm diameter
- A short piece, around 5cm long of 1-2mm wire – I buy this from garden centres or DIY shops

Additional tool needed for the pendants:
- 6mm or 7mm diameter knitting needle

CLAY:

For the orange coloured pendant and mushroom blend I used:
- Cernit metalic green & bronze
- Premo gold, pearl & copper

For the blue coloured pendant and mushroom blend I used:
- Cernit metalic green & turquoise
- Premo pearl & silver
- Also need black clay for both

Mica shift is a technique that creates a 3D effect on a flat piece of clay. Metallic clay has mica (metal) particles in it, and by manipulating these particles in this technique, you get the two-toned 'ghost' effect.

FINISHING:

You have the option of leaving them with just a light sanding, sanding and polishing to a high sheen, or varnishing.

Sanding and polishing:
- 1000 grit wet and dry sandpaper
- Set of 6 micromesh sheets in 1500, 1800, 2400, 3600, 6000 and 12000 grit
- Rennaisance wax

Varnishing:
- You can use any polymer clay varnish, but I use Darwi Vernis, which comes in gloss or satin

Making the blend:

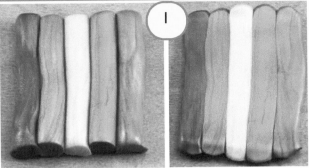

Roll out logs of clay, 1cm diameter x 5cm long
Cernit Bronze, Premo Copper, Premo Pearl,
Premo Gold, Cernit metallic Green.
Flatten slightly with a the clay roller.

Fold the clay over, slightly offsetting it as shown. You don't want to offset too much or you'll lose the original colours once it's blended. Put it through the pasta machine, folded side first, and continuing to fold, keeping the green one side and the bronze the other, and putting through the pasta machine on PM0 until you have a smooth blend.

The finished blend.
Now put it through the pasta machine on PM1, PM2 and PM3.

Make sure, when making the blend thinner, that you don't make the stripes wider. Put it through with the stripes going vertically through the pasta machine.

For this blend use:
- Premo Pearl
- Cernit metallic Green
- Premo Silver
- Premo Pearl
- Cernit Turquoise

Adding the mica shift:

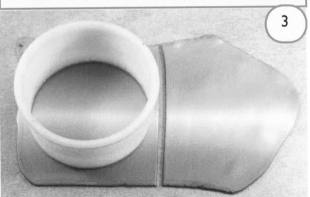

Using a 6cm circle as a guide, cut the blend in two. If you want to make the mushroom, use the piece on the left. I'm going to start with the pendant, so use the smaller piece on the right.

Dust the clay with some cornflour (also known as cornstarch) and get a deep texture sheet. I've used a Melanie Murr design here.

141

This is how I keep my cornflour. I put it in two layers of muslin and tie an elastic band round it to make a little pouch. Then, because I don't want cornflour everywhere, I keep it in a bowl.

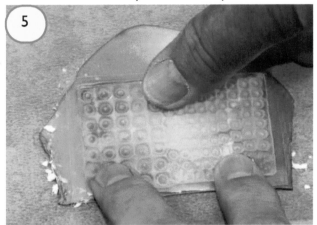

5

Many people like to use their roller to push the texture sheet into the clay, but I never have much success with that, it always seems to move. I use two fingers to hold the texture sheet in place, and with my thumb, press firmly down all over the sheet. You can also use the pad at the base of your thumb to do this if you want more pressure.

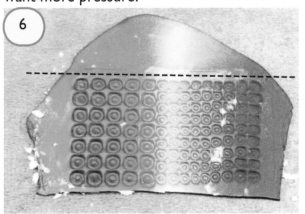

6

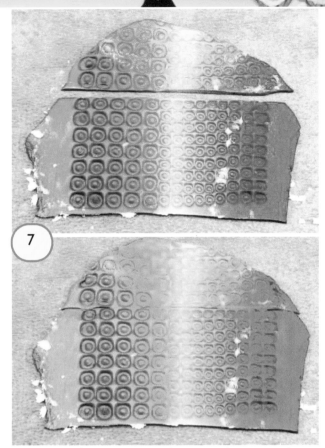

7

Because the texture sheet isn't quite large enough for the pendant, you need to make another piece to add on.

If you just move the texture sheet and press down again you will get a mark from the edge of the sheet. Instead, cut along where shown in the previous photograph, texture the cut off piece, trim that piece and add it to the first. Don't smooth the join or you'll lose the deep texture.

Now for the fun part!

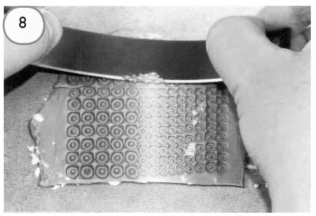

8

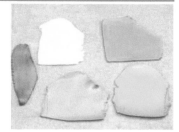

With your flexible tissue blade, hold it firmly with both hands and curve it by pushing down with both thumbs. Start at the back of the piece, place the blade just behind some of the pattern and carefully slice towards you, removing the raised parts of clay. I like to rest my hands on the work surface to keep the blade from going too deep into the clay.

It's best to do short slices until you're confident in the technique, and most importantly, carefully brush or blow off the loose clay after EVERY slice, otherwise you'll have little bits of clay embedded into your design. Carry on until the whole of the area is smooth, with all raised parts sliced off.

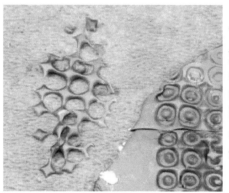

The slices you take off can sometimes be used in designs of their own.

(9)

Once you have taken off all the top layer of the texture, cover your clay with deli paper - you can also use greaseproof paper, layout paper, or even just plain white printer paper - and burnish well with your chosen burnisher. Don't worry too much about any areas that aren't as good as you like, you can put the circle designs there and cover them!

Adding the circles:

(10)

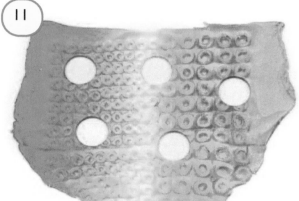

Lay your textured clay sheet on some deli paper and roll out some of the five colours used in the blend on PM3.

(11)

I always start with the largest circles, in this case it's an 11mm diameter Kemper cutter, and cut out some circles. It might be a good idea to lightly mark the shape of your pendant before you start putting in the circles. I've sometimes made a lovely circle design, only to find that it's impossible to make a nice pendant shape without cutting a circle in half.

(12)

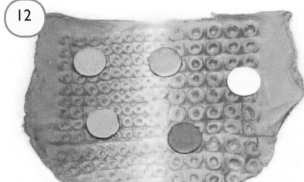

Cut some 11mm circles from the pieces of clay you rolled out earlier, and put them in the holes. Before you place them in, turn them over, this makes a neater fit.

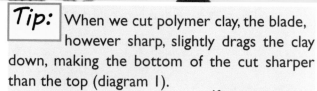

If we put two pieces of clay together which have both been cut from the top, there will be a small gap (diagram 2).

However, if you turn one of the pieces (diagram 3), the two pieces will fit far better together, with no gap. I've used wine glasses to show the original way up the clay is when cut.

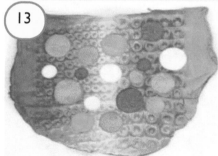

Once you've put the large holes in, go a size smaller, I used 9mm, then finally the small size 6mm.

You don't have to use these sizes, or even use different sizes, they could all be the same size circles, whatever you prefer. Once you are happy with the amount of circles you have, burnish it well.

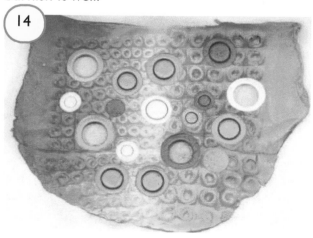

Once well burnished, it's time to take out the middles. I've used 8mm, 7mm and 4mm. Give the cutter a little twist to make a really good cut, and I use the tip of my craft knife to get the middles out.

Roll out some black clay on PM4, then texture it. I use a thin piece of sponge, but you could use sandpaper, or even something like scrunched up paper or a toothbrush. It's not imperative you texture the sheet for this part, I just like the look of it behind the circles.

Tip: Before you place the blended sheet on the black clay, carefully remove any rough edges in the circles. I do this by turning the blend over so you're looking at the back, and gently using a finger to smooth the inside of the circles, removing any little rough edges and stray bits of clay, which will really show against the black background.

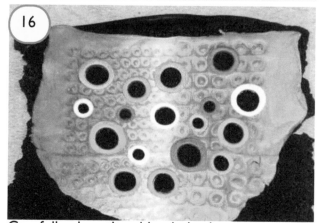

Carefully lay the blended sheet onto the textured side of the black clay. Make sure there are no air pockets, and handle it carefully as otherwise you'll distort the holes.

Making the pendant:

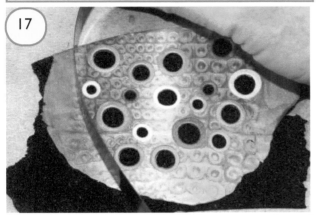

17

Taking your flexible tissue blade, curve it and cut one of the pendant sides. Repeat all round the pendant. Alternatively you could use a pre-made cutter, or even design your own, cut it out from card, lay on the clay and cut round.

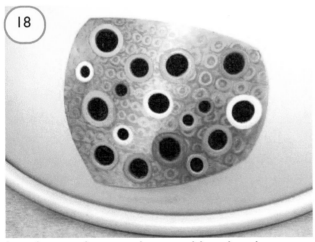

18

Lay the pendant on the metal bowl and cure for 1 hour at the clay manufacturer's recommended temperature.

19

Once cured and cool, cover the back with clay adhesive.

20

Make another sheet of black textured clay on PM4 and cover the back of the pendant, then use your craft knift to cut off the excess all the way round, leaving some to cover the edges.

21

Holding the pendant with the texture sheet, gently push the clay up onto the edge of the pendant all the way round.

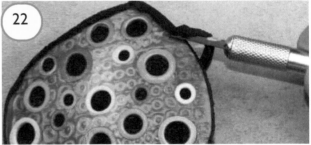

22

With your craft knife, cut off the excess clay.

To make the bail you'll need a 6mm or 7mm needle, some cornflour, and textured black clay on PM2.

23

Cut a piece of clay, the width you want the bail to be. I've used a diamond shaped cutter, but you can use a circle, square or rectangle, any shape that can be folded over. Cover the needle with some cornflour and fold the clay over it,

24

Place the bail on the back of the pendant and press down gently. Remove the needle and use the texture to remove any indentations left by the needle on the edge of the pendant.

25

Place the pendant, pattern side down, in some cornflour. If you don't have this, you can put it on paper, but the cornflour is good as it takes the shape of the pendant and helps it keep its curve. Cure for 30 mins at the same temperature as before.

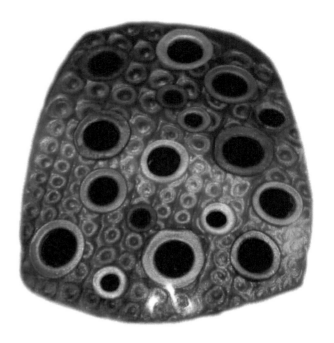

Using the 600 grit sandpaper, sand all over. You can then either leave it as it is, varnish it with polymer clay varnish, or, my preference, sand and polish to a high sheen.

To do this I use 600 grit wet and dry sandpaper, then 1000 grit. After this I use a set of 6 micromesh sheets on 1500, 1800, 2400, 3600, 6000 & 12000 grit. Wash the pendant and each sheet before moving on to the next one.

Finally I use rennaissance wax and buff to a high sheen with a dremel, or a rough material like denim or towel.

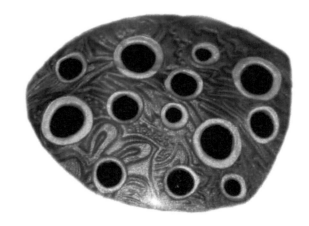

The blue blend pendant.

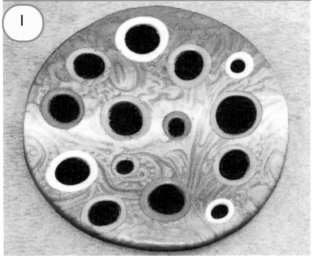

Take the remaining piece of blend and lightly press the 6cm circle cutter into it, you only want to see where the cutter is going, as a guide to where you're going to put the spots, not cut it. Follow the instructions for the pendant to make the holes and back it. If you look carefully, you can see I haven't removed the excess clay round the holes, which really show against the black background. Obviously this is a case of do as I say, not what I do!!

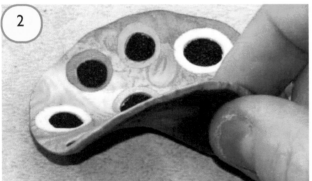

Now pinch all the way round the circle to make a nice thin edge. When you're pinching, use your finger on the hole side and your thumb underneath. As you pinch, slightly move your thumb towards the inside of the circle. This will make the edge thinner, but also push the black clay inwards, so you are left with a rim of the coloured clay, underneath, which makes a nicer looking edge when finished.

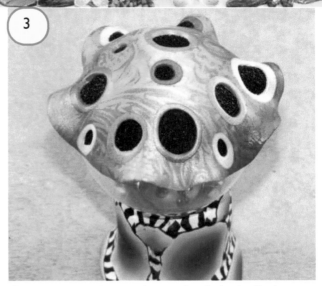

Gently place the circle on the light bulb. As you can see I've made a base for the light bulb and covered with purple canes, but if you don't want to do this you can put the light bulb in a toilet roll middle instead. Carefully ease the clay round the bulb, leaving a wavy edge; this is totally personal preference, you may want it completely touching the bulb like a little dome, or you may want it more open and wavy as I've done here. Cure for I hour at the clay manufacturers recommended temperature. I cure cernit and premo at 130°C.

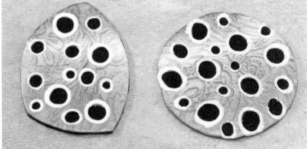

This is the pendant and mushroom from the blue blend. I made a mistake on the one on the right, I forgot to burnish the clay before cutting the middle holes out, so had to burnish afterwards which distorted the holes. However, as this was for the mushroom, I decided that I quite liked the effect as it was more organic and natural looking. On the mushrooms I've used a texture sheet from Cernit, their texture sheets are also lovely and deep.

As you can see, with the blue mushroom I've eased it tightly onto the light bulb, making more of a dome shaped mushroom.

Spread clay adhesive over the whole of the underside of the mushroom and lay the spotty circle on it, easing it into all the curves.

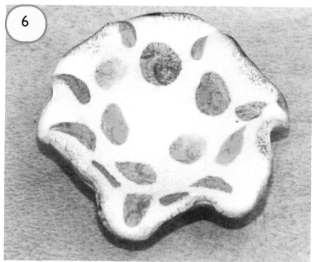

6

Gently pinch all round the edges to make a smooth join. I've pinched a little enthusiastically as you can see the black clay undernearth. Maybe don't do it quite as much as me! Cure for 30 minutes. I like to put it in cornflour.

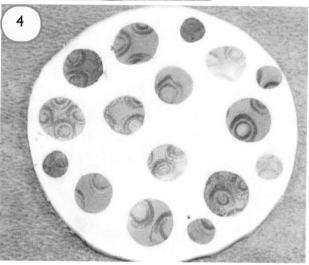

4

Once cured, make the underside of the mushroom by rolling out some pearl clay on PM3, and inserting the cut out clay from the pendant or mushroom top. You can use any clay, but I think these tie the underneath nicely with the top. Burnish well then cut out a 6cm

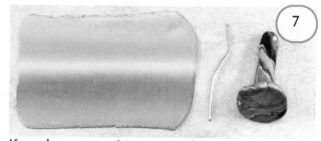

7

If you're not making a pendant, use the other half of the blend for the mushroom stalk. Otherwise make another blend, with the same clay, but half the amount. Roll the clay to PM5.

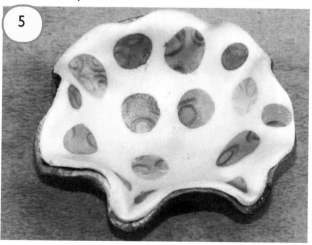

5

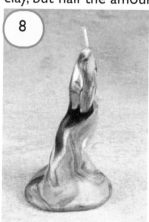

8

For the stalk you'll need the blend, a piece of 1-2mm wire, and some scrap clay.

Cut the wire to measure around 1cm longer than the height of your stalk. Roll the scrap clay into a stalk shape and insert the wire.

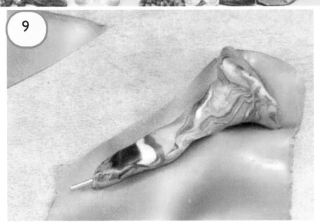

9

Lay the stalk on the blend at an angle, you want the colours to wind up the stalk rather than just go round it horizontally.

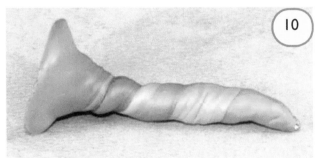

10

Cut the blend to size and smooth the join. Next twist the whole stalk as shown.

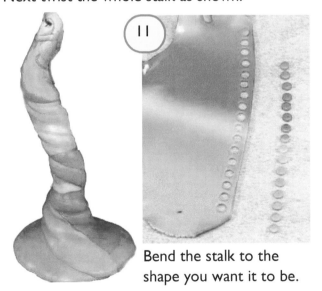

11

Bend the stalk to the shape you want it to be.

Then talk the remaining blend, roll it out to a thin setting, and cut out small circles. Use these to decorate your stalk. You can do what you like regarding this, texture it, put stripes, spots, holes, twisted clay, whatever takes your fancy.

12

Put your stalk on a small tile to decorate and cure. This makes it easier to add embellishments and keep it the shape you want.

For the blue blend mushroom I've made mini mushrooms and put them on the base of the stalk.

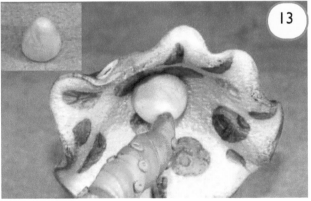

13

Roll a small cone of clay (see insert), put some clay adhesive in the middle of the underside of the mushroom, and push on the cone.

Insert the piece of wire at the top of the stalk into the cone and push well in. Put the whole mushroom in the oven and cure for another hour.

149

GALLERY

150

3 Christmas Robin Tree Decorations :

TOOLS & MATERIALS:

- Pasta Machine
- Tissue blade – flexible
- Clay roller
- Tile to work on
- Oven to cure your robins in
- Aluminium tin foil
- 2.5cm and 3cm heart cutters
- 3cm circle cutter
- 3 x cocktail sticks
- Large knitting needle
- Polymer clay adhesive
- Deli wrap or white paper for burnishing
- Burnishing tool. I use a soap stone. but a smooth stone or just your finger will do
- Ultra fine glitter in gold or any colour – optional
- 6 x 4mm black glass beads for eyes
- Polymer clay varnish – optional

THREADING MATERIALS:

- Tiger tail or other beading wire
- 9 crimps. 3 for each robin
- 20 seeds beads per robin, or two long tube beads per robin for the legs
- About 5 beads per robin to decorate the hanging wire
- Wire cutters
- Flat nosed pliers

CLAY:

- 1/2 x 56g block of Premo Accents Copper
- 1/2 x 56g block of Premo Accents Bronze
- 1 x 56g block of Premo Accents Pearl
- 1 x 56g block of Premo Burnt Umber
- 1/2 x 56g block of Premo Pomegranate
- 1/2 x 56g block of Premo Black
- 1/4 x 56g block of Premo White
- 1/4 x 56g block of Premo Yellow
- 1/4 x 56g block of Premo Gold
- Scrap clay approximately 1/2 x 56g block

THREE CANES:

Making the robin body:

Take a piece of tin foil, 15cm x 15cm, and roll loosely into a ball, before pressing more firmly into a more compact ball

Roll some scrap clay on PM2 and cut 2 x 3cm circles for each ball. Cover the balls and roll in your hands to smooth out the joins. Make sure you don't have any air bubbles; if you do, make a small slit with your blade and push the air out. If you don't have a circle cutter, just use pieces of clay rolled at PM2.

Robin body cane:

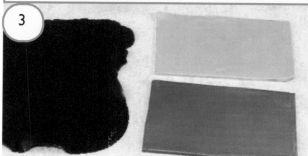

Roll the copper clay and the bronze clay on PM2 and cut each to the size of a standard playing card - 6cm x 9cm. Roll some black clay on a thin setting, around PM7.

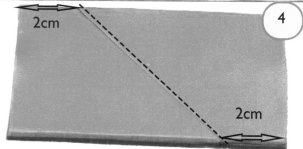

Stack the copper on top of the bronze, mark 2cm from the top left corner and 2cm from the bottom right corner, and cut between.

Separate the pieces and stack copper on copper and bronze on bronze.

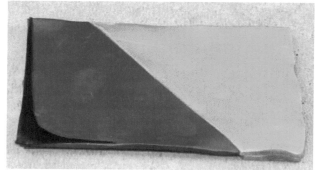

Cut a piece of the thin black clay as shown. Put it over the end of the bronze clay. This darkens one side to make a better contrast.

Follow instruction on page * to make a Skinner blend.

152

Fold the sheet in half but this time put it through the pasta machine with either the copper or bronze shorter unfolded end first, making a longer, thinner strip. Put through again on PM2.

Roll some pearl clay on PM0 and cut it the same width as the copper/bronze strip, and a third of the length.

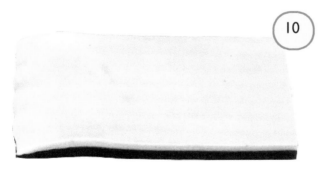

Roll out some burnt umber also on PM0, lay the pearl clay on top and cut round.

Lay the copper/bronze blend on top of the pearl side of the strip you've just made. Cut the excess pearl/burnt umber off.

Roll up tightly, starting at the copper end, with the burnt umber on the outside.

Pinch the end of the cane before finishing the roll, this makes a neater, more natural join. Press the cane firmly to help all the layers stick together, then roll it to lengthen until it measures 1.5cm in diameter.

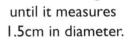

Cut thin slices, around 1mm thick, off the cane and put them round the robin body.

Pinch one of the short ends before putting through the pasta machine on PM0, short end first. Then repeat at PM2 and PM3. This will make a long, thin piece of two-tone clay.

Place the slices as close as possible to each other, it doesn't matter if they overlap a little. Once coverered, use your fingers to gently push the cane slices together so none of the scrap clay is visible. Finally roll the ball in your hands to smooth all the joins.

Tartan cane:

Start by rolling out and conditioning the pomegranate clay and cutting 3 x 3cm circles (the ones on the left hand side), and stack in a column.

Cut ten more circles in pomegranate, put them together into a sheet and add a very small amount of black clay to the ten circles. Mix and keep adding tiny amounts of black clay until you have a slightly darker red; cut 6 x 3cm circles (the ones in the middle two rows), stack in two columns.

Finally add further tiny amounts of black clay to the remaining medium red clay until you have a slightly darker colour again, then cut 3 x 3cm circles (right hand side) and stack.

Roll each column of three circles into a ball, you will end up with four balls of clay, one red, two slightly darker red, and one darkeat red. Make each ball into a cube, then pull out all 8 corners as shown in the middle picture. Now roll with your clay roller each side and you will have a cube with good sharp corners. Do this with all four balls.

Put the four cubes together as shown. The two medium red cubes (M) diagonally to each other.

Roll some yellow clay on PM4. Make a cut along one side, cutting a third of the way up to the middle.

Place the piece you've cut off, cut side down onto the yellow clay.
Trim the yellow round the red clay and replace onto the block.

Repeat on the other three sides, making sure that you keep looking at the underside to make sure that the lines are straight and look the same as the top.

Repeat step 20, with black clay, again on PM4, slightly inside the yellow lines. Make sure you continue to look underneath, it is really important that both sides look the same.

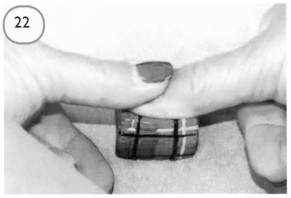

To lengthen the cane, I like to use my thumbs to press on all four sides, then gently pull. Repeat this until the cane is long enough to use your roller to lengthen.

Lenghten to 16cm, cut off any distorted ends and roll again to 16cm.
Cut into 4 x 4cm pieces.

Put the four pieces together, making sure that the patterns match, ie in the cane above, the dark square is in the top left of each of the four pieces.
Roll the cane until you have the size of tartan you want.

Making the front of the robin:

Condition and roll some white clay on PM6.
Cut three 3cm hearts.
You'll notice that each heart has a little 'step' on the left side, this is the cutter. I like to smooth out any cutter marks or rough edges.

155

Roll some red clay on PM4. With a 2.5cm cutter, make marks but don't actually cut the clay. This is so you can see how much of the clay sheet you need to cover with the tartan.

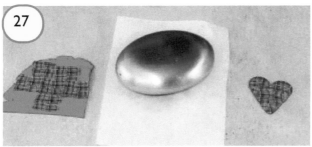

Cut thin slices of the tartan cane and place them on the red clay, covering the heart mark. Put some deli wrap, greaseproof or layout paper over and burnish. Burnishing is rubbing with a small tool, I use a soap stone, over paper which smooths out any uneven bits and makes the joins disappear.
Finally cut a 2.5cm heart from each piece.

Place the tartan heart on top of the white heart. I like to make the top of the two pieces level, but this is purely the way I do it.; you may prefer to have more white showing at the top. Put the heart on the robin body. If there are any unevenly covered parts, that's a good place to put the heart!

Gently press the hearts down on the robin, then insert 2 x 4mm black glass beads for eyes. Push them well in. If you don't have beads, you can use little balls of black clay.

Form the beack by rolling a ball of gold clay the size of a small pea, then roll each end between first finger and thumb to make the 'rugby ball' shape. Do not make too thin, it will break.

Make a hole with a knitting needle where you want the beak to be. Put some Bake & Bond in the hole. Gently push one end of your beak into the hole, make two small holes with the needle tool for nostrils, and a cut with your blade to make the two halves of the beak.

Finally push a cocktail stick through the robin to show how it's going to hang,; it also provide stability for when you put the tail and wings on.

Making the wings & tail cane:

32

Roll Premo Pearl and Premo Burnt Umber on PM2 and cut to the size of a standard playing card 9cm x 6cm. Roll some black clay on PM7 and add a curved piece, as shown. Make a Skinner blend as you did for the robin body cane.

33

Cut into three equal pieces.

34

Stack the three pieces and roll gently with your clay roller to adhere them. Pinch one of the short ends, it can be either end. Put through the pasta machine, short end first, on PM0, PM2, PM4 & PM6 to make a long, thin strip. Roll up, pearl end first.

35

Cover the cane with a thin layer of black clay, rolled on PM7. See page * for how to do this.

36

Lenthen the cane to 10cm, trim any distorted ends, and roll again to 10cm. Cut a 4cm piece.

37

Flatten the 4cm piece to a width of 2cm.

Lengthen and cut the remaining cane as follows:

Roll the 6cm remaining piece to 8cm, cut a 4cm piece and flatten to 1.5cm.

Roll the remaining 4cm piece to 6cm, cut a 4cm piece and flatten to 1cm.

Slightly flatten the remaining 2cm piece.

Stack the four pieces as shown in the picture to the right.

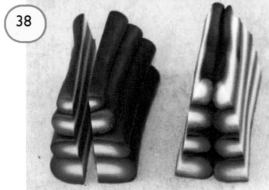

38

Cut the stack through the middle as shown in the picture on the left, then put each piece 'back-to-back', as shown in the picture on the right.

39

Lengthen the cane, keeping it in a triangular shape, to 8cm, cut off the distorted ends and lengthen again to 8cm. I like to cover the cane in ultra fine glitter. The picture on the right shows silver and gold ultra fine glitter.

40

Cut a 2mm slice and place on the robin at the back in the middle. Then cut 2 thinner slices, 1mm thick, and place at the sides for the wings. It's important to place the tail piece first as it makes it easier to position the wings evenly.

Wings can be placed either with the pointed end to the front, or the more square end, it's totally up to you which you prefer.

Making the hats:

41

Roll 2 x 3cm circles on PM0. Pinch round the endges of one, this is going to be the rim of the hat.

Roll the other one first into a ball, then into a cylinder shape.

Place the cylinder on top of the flattened circle.

42

Decorate your hat any way you like. I've put a band of tartan round the left one, two leaves and three red berries on the middle hat, and the hat on the right is a ball of scrap clay covered with thin slices of the tartan clay, flattened, and a ball of black on top to look like a Scottish hat.

However, if preferred you can leave your robin without at hat, it is totally up to you.

Making the feet:

43

Roll some gold clay into a log 3mm diameter. For each robin cut 2 x 2.5cm and 2 x 2cm. Round the end of each peice, make the 2.5cm pieces into a horseshoe shape, then place the 2cm piece in the middle, as shown in the picture on the right.

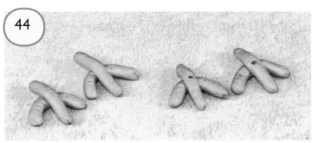

44

Make lines along each of the toes, then with your needle tool make a hole through the middle of each foot.

Cure the robins and the feet for an hour at the clay manufacturers recommended temperature.

Threading the robins:

45

For each robin you will need around 42cm of threading wire, 3 crimps, assorted beads for above the robin, either 20 seed beads or two tube beads for the legs, a pair of wire cutters and a pair of flat nosed pliers.

46

Thread a crimp bead on both ends of the wire and close 6cm from the folded end. Thread assorted beads on next; there is no need to put another crimp bead on.

47

Thread both pieces of wire through the robin; you may need to make the hole a little larger, I use my needle tool to do this. On each leg thread either 10 seed beads or one tube bead. Thread the foot on making sure the side with the ridges on are uppermost, then finish with a crimp bead, and snip off excess wire. You can now varnish your robin, and it's completed.

Alternative red breast:

Instead of the tartan, you can use a roller such as a Kor roller to make a pattern, and highlight with metallic paste.

159

Christmas Tea-lights:

TOOLS & MATERIALS:

- Pasta machine
- Tissue blade
- Craft knife • Ruler
- Oven to cure clay in
- Tile to work on
- Acrylic or metal clay roller
- Needle tool / cocktail stick
- Knitting needle for blending joins
- Small ball tool
- Deli wrap or white paper for burnishing
- Soapstone. bone folder. smooth stone. credit card. or anything else to burnish with
- Circle cutters 2cm. 15mm & 1cm
- Sandpaper. texture sheet or a sponge to texture white clay
- Glasses or glass tea-light holders. I use rounded shot glasses from Sainsburys
- Glass painting outliner in white and brown . I use pebeo – water based
- If you want to varnish the tea-lights you will need polymer clay varnish. I use Darwi Vernis

CLAY – for each light:

- Around 1/4 of a 56g block of white. green & yellow
- Small amounts of copper. red. orange. gold. brown & black
- Slices of the robin tree decoration canes pg *

Gallery:

I've used black card in the tea-lights to show the designs better

The snow:

Roll some white clay on PM3 and cut a rectangular shape long enough to go round the glass you are decorating and twice the height required. Texture the clay using a sponge, or anything you might have.

With a craft knife, cut a wavy line all the way along the strip.

Wrap one half of the stripe round the bottom of the glass, straight edge down, and overlap. Then cut through both pieces on the overlapped part.

Take off the two excess parts either side of the cut and join the strip.

Finally, using a craft knife, trim the top of the piece that is higher than the other so that it makes a seamless wave. Smooth over the join with a knitting need and re-texture.

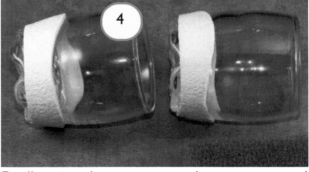

Finally, using the sponge, or whatever you used to texture, press it gently along the edge of the white clay. The glass on the right has had this done, it makes a more natural looking snow.

Snowmen:

Roll out white clay on PM3 and texture.

There are several texture sheets you can buy, I use ones from Helen Briel (grey, right), Cernit (orange, left), and a recent one called a Clay Squisher from Judi Kins. Alternatively, you do not need a commercial texture plate, you can use a sponge, some wire wool, sandpaper, anthing really to make some texture.

If using a commercial texture, set your pasta machine at the thickest setting, either spray the sheet with alcohol or water (I use gin!) or dust with cornflour, and put it throught the pasta machine with the sheet of clay.

Cut two circles, 15mm for the body and 1cm for the head.

Place on the snow, make sure that the large circle is slightly overlapping the snow. I usually put two snowmen on each glass.

To make the scarf, roll some clay, colour of choice, on PM3 and cut 5 pieces, 4cm x 2cm. Roll the second colour on PM3, place the 5

pieces on it, and cut round them. You now have 5 pieces of the two colours, stack as shown. Cut the stack into 5mm slices.

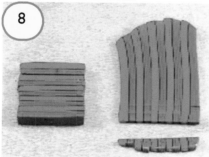

Put each slice through the pasta machine on PM0, stripes vertical.

Making sure that the stripes go through vertically, (facing down) ensures that the stripes don't get any wider. Put through again on PM2.

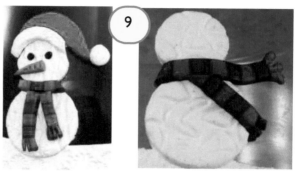

Cut a couple of pieces off to make the scarf, and when placed, make two little cuts in the ends of the scarf.

To make the bobble hat, roll out some red clay on PM3 and using a 1cm circle, make a circular mark. Using a craft knife, cut a hat shape, using the shape of the circle for the bottom. For the hat trim and bobble, roll some white clay on PM0, cut a 3mm strip and a 5mm circle. Put on the snowman as shown. Texture with a small ball tool.

For the eyes and buttons use balls of black clay. For the nose, roll some orange clay into a carrot shape, and make little lines on it.

To make a top hat, roll some black clay on PM3 and cut 15mm x 2mm for the rim and 8mm x 8mm for the top of the hat.

The hat can be decorated with leaves and berries, a strip of the scarf cane, tartan, or left plain. Refer to the robin tree decoration tutorial for how to make leaves and a tartan cane.

Trees:

Take three different colours of clay, whatever colours you want your trees to be in. I've used dark green, light green and gold, and roll a log of each, 6cm long, 1cm diameter. Gently flatten then put through the pasta machine on PM0.
Fold into half, slightly offsetting it, and put it through the pasta machine again. Continue to fold in half andn put through until you have an even blend.

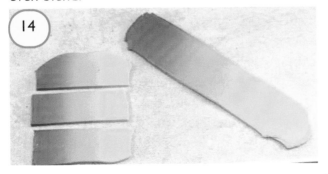

Cut the blend into three (left on picture 14) and stack them (not shown). Pinch one of the short ends and put through the pasta machine, pinched short end first, at PM0 (right on picture 14) then PM2, PM4 and PM6.

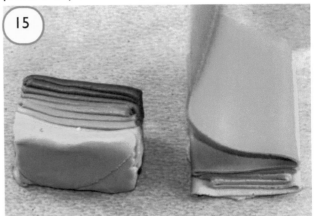

To make a 'plug', fold the clay in a fan fold, zig-zagging in 3cm wide folds, until the whole strip is folded and in a block, I call a plug.

Lengthen your cane by rolling it on each side with a clay roller and gently pulling until it is around three times as long. Cut into three equal pieces. If preferred you can cut it into more, I often use 6 - see picture at the end of step 19.

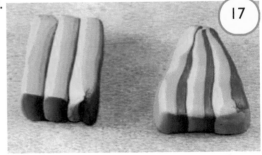

Stack the three (or more) pieces on top of each other and pinch on one end as shown.

163

1.5cm

Lengthen the cane until the base of the triangle measures 1.5cm. Cut the cane in half and put one half to one side. Lengthen the other piece until the base reaches 12mm, cut two thirds off and put to one side. Lengthen the remaining third to 1cm; you now have three canes which will make the trees. Cut a 1mm slice of each.

Place the largest triangle on first, then place the second one slightly overlapping it, then the smallest one on top.

To make the tree trunk cut a rectangle of brown clay. Make sure that the tree trunk is touching the snow.

Left: I like to put a gold star on top of the tree. You can also decorate it with balls of coloured clay.
Below: the tree cane made by cutting it into 6.

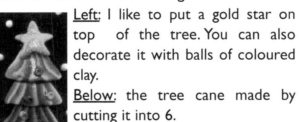

Robins:

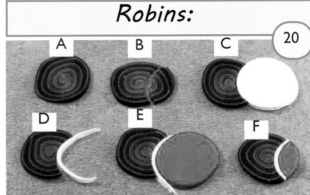

The robin body is made using the cane from the robin tree decoration on page 152.

A. Cut a slice 2cm diameter and 2mm thick.
B. Using a 2cm circle cutter, cut about 1/3rd of the cane slice off
C. Roll some white clay on PM3, cut a 2cm circle and push it into the brown cane slice. Take some deli wrap or white paper, lay it over the white and cane slice and burnish to adhere the two clays.

D.

D. With the 2cm circle cutter make another cut, leaving a small amount of white behind
E. Roll some red clay on PM3, cut a 2cm circle and push next to the white clay. Burnish
F. With a craft knife, cut the excess white and red clay off to make a circle

For the tails I use the wing cane from the robin tree decorations, page *. You can also use this for the wing (left picture), or you can roll some copper clay on PM3 and cut a 1cm oval. Pull into a leaf shape and mark some leaf vein lines as shown. For the eyes use small balls of black clay and for the beak use gold clay on PM3 cut into a triangle. You can also use the tartan cane for the breast (right).

Place the robins on the snow. For the legs, roll gold clay into very thin logs and make legs as shown.

(22)

Once you've put on all the clay decorations, cure your clay at the clay manufacturers recommended temperature, for 45 minutes. Let cool before the final decoration.

Final decoration:

To make the snow flakes and the snowmen's arms I use a white and a brown (or copper) glass painting outliner. As well as the snow flakes, you can put snow on top of the hats.

The mistletoe was made by a light to dark green skinner blend, rolled into a bulls eye cane, with the light in the middle, then squashed into a leaf shape. The glass has black card in the middle so you can see the design more effectively.

As clay does not stick to glass, it is important that no decoration is on its own, there needs to be a ring of clay all the way round the glass, and the mistletoe is attached to a ring of snow at the top.

Similarly with the tree baubles tea-light, the ribbon of gold round the top anchors the rest to the glass.

Finally, I like to varnish the clay with my favourite polymer clay varnish, Darwi Vernis, but this is totally optional.

Tea-lights can be put in many different glasses, try looking round the charity shops, taking a couple of different sizes of tea lights with you to make sure they fit.

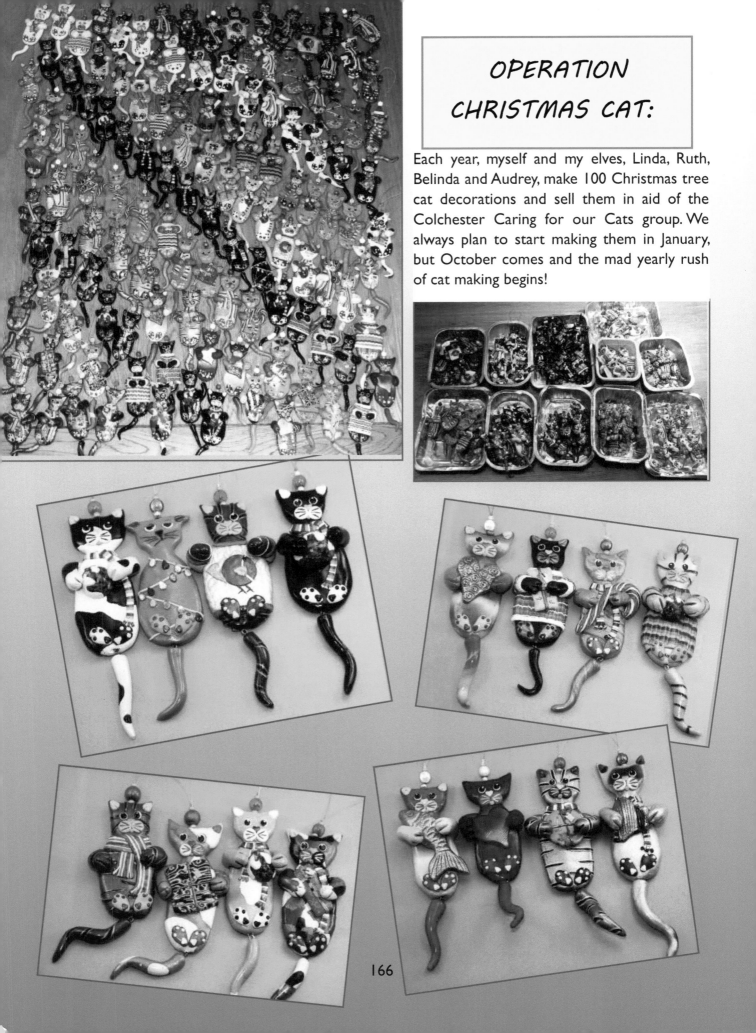

OPERATION CHRISTMAS CAT:

Each year, myself and my elves, Linda, Ruth, Belinda and Audrey, make 100 Christmas tree cat decorations and sell them in aid of the Colchester Caring for our Cats group. We always plan to start making them in January, but October comes and the mad yearly rush of cat making begins!

Christmas Cat tree decorations:

These Christmas tree decorations were designed to sell in aid of a group called 'Colchester Caring for our Cats' in Colchester. During the Covid-19 pandemic my cat Casper got out of his cage at the vet's and went missing for a month. The group gave me advice, support, and encouragement, and I eventually got him back. I made around 150 cats and all sales went to the group who work tirelessly to rescue, rehome, and protect the cats of Colchester. I hope you have as much fun making them as I did.

TOOLS & MATERIALS:

- Pasta machine
- Tissue blade
- Craft knife • Ruler
- Oven to cure clay in
- Tile to work on
- Acrylic or metal clay roller
- Needle tool / cocktail stick
- Deli wrap
- Soap stone for burnishing – or a smooth stone. bone folder or credit card can also be used
- Circle cutter 1cm & 4cm
- A variety of small circle cutters. or some Ferrule bootlace crimps – see separate box on the right
- 3/16" triangle and heart shape cutters – optional. you don't need them. I just find them nice for the nose
- Bead piercing pins 1.7mm diameter – or you could use a 2mm metal knitting needle or cocktail sticks.
- Alternatively you could use 2 x 7mm rings or wire for each cat instead

TOOLS. MATERIALS CONT:

- Small screw eye pins 4mm x 8mm. One per cat
- Nail art transfers – optional
- Large knitting needle for burnishing
- If you want to varnish the cat you will need polymer clay varnish. I use Darwi Vernis

Threading material:

- Pliers and wire cutters
- Tiger tail beading wire. or any beading wire for hanging
- Superglue
- Hand drill with 1mm drill bit
- Jewellry crimps. one per cat

Clay:

- You will need some scrap clay for the middle of the cats. and whatever coloured clay you want to use for the colour of your cat and the decorations

Ferrule bootlace crimps:

- I use Ferrule bootlace crimps – you can buy them on ebay or electrical shops. These are great as they come in a variety of sizes and can also be made into other shapes. The ones I use for the cats are 1mm. 2mm. 3mm. 4mm. 5mm. 6mm & 7mm.
I use the 4mm to make into a triangular shape for the feet. and the 7mm to make an inner ear shape. but you don't need these. you can easily cut the shapes out by hand. it's just easier.

Making the basic cat:

Roll some scrap clay on PM0 and cut out 2 x 4cm circles. Roll them together into a ball and then a log shape measuring 6cm long.

Roll some clay (whatever colour you want to make your cat) on PM3. Place the log on it and cut a straight line along one long edge of the log and two straight lines around 3mm away from the short ends. You need the 3mm extra to be able to cover the ends of the log.

Roll the clay round the log until the straight end reaches the clay, then roll a little further. When you roll it back you will see a line; cut along this line. The two edges will then meet.

Fold the extra clay at each end inwards and roll on the work surface to smooth.

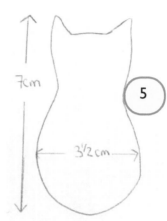

Draw a cat shape, roughly the dimensions shown on the left as this makes a nice thickness of cat. If you want to make a larger one, use more clay; smaller, use less clay.

I'm going to show you two ways of making a cat, using different threading methods. The first way is to push a bead piercing pin through your clay log lengthways. There are two thicknesses of piercing pins, make sure it's the thicker one. Alternatively you could thread a thin skewer or knitting needle instead, up to 2mm diameter, or a cocktail stick. Roll the log to make sure it's smooth all over.

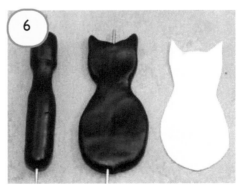

Pinch the log 2cm from one end; this is going to be the neck. Then by either keeping the cat on the work surface and pressing down, or holding it in the air between both fingers and thumbs, gently manipulate the clay into the cat shape pulling out the ears. I find it easier to have a cardboard shape already cut out to measure the cat against as I go along.

168

The second way to prepare your cat for threading is to make it into a cat shape, then use either a 7mm metal ring, or some wire made into a ring. Cut a slit in the bottom of your cat, insert the ring in half way, then press firmly and smooth the join to secure the ring.

Do the same at the top of the head, but put the ring the other way round, this is so when you add the thread the cat will face forwards.

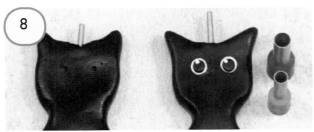

To make the eyes, first use your needle tool to mark where you want the eyes to be, then roll some black and white clay on PM6, and using the 5mm cutter cut two circles out in white, then two black circles with the 4mm cutter. Place them on the cat, and finally roll two tiny amounts of white clay and put them on the top left of each eye.

As you can see, playing about with where you place the black circle can give the cat a completely different expression. And you don't

have to stick with circular eyes, or black and white. For the cat on the right I've used an oval cutter first, filled with a mixture of green and translucent clay, then added two thin black lines instead of dots.

For the nose roll some clay on PM3 (I've used some silver mixed with black) and cut a heart shape, or a triangle.

Cat's ears are usually lighter in colour, even the black ones, so I roll some of the silver/black blend on PM7 and cut a shape for the middle of the ears. You can do this by hand, or do what I've done, bend a 1cm ferrule bootlace crimp to the shape I want. To finish make an indentation in the bottom half of each ear.

For the mouth you can either make little puff balls (am I the only person who calls the cheeks that?), or make indentations with your needle tool and back fill after curing. For the puff balls roll some clay on PM0 and cut two 6mm circles, roll them into balls, then flatten slightly before placing them either side of the nose. Add a little triangle of pink clay to make the mouth, and finally make three lines in each puff ball for whiskers.

For the other two cats I've used my needle tool to make the shape of the mouth, and added little holes either side, which when backfilled will look like little whisker holes.

For the tail roll a 4cm tapered log, 7mm to 3mm. It can be straight, wavy or curled.

To make the back feet, for each cat roll clay on PM0 and cut two 1cm circles. Roll them into balls then into a flattened teardrop shape. Push the edge of your needle tool into the rounded part in three places to look like toes.

Roll some clay on PM7 in the colour you want the toes and pad to be and cut 6 x 1mm circles, and 2 triangles. Again I've made a custom-made cutter from a 4mm ferrule crimp, but you can easily roll tiny balls instead of the 1mm cutter, and cut a triangle shape by hand.

For the all-black cat, black feet wouldn't show so I've used the silver/black mix with black toes and pads.

To add other colours, roll some clay (I've used white) on PM7, cut out the shape, then using your needle tool, make little lines from the white to the black to look like hair.

Making the jumper:

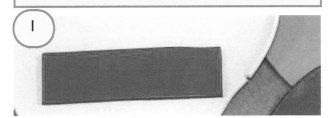

I've used three colours for my jumper, Premo Pomegranite, Premo Bright Green Pearl, and Premo White. Roll them all on PM3 and cut out 2 x rectangles of each, 6cm x 2.5cm; then stack them, red/white/green/red/white/green.

I do this by cutting just one rectangle out in the first colour (pomegranite), then laying it on the second colour (white) and cutting round it, then repeating with the third colour (green). Repeat once more with each colour and you end up with your stack.

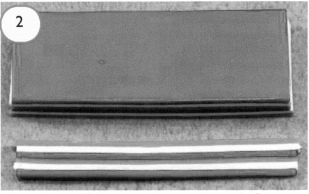

Cut a slice off the stack, approximately 2mm.

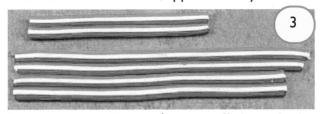

Next put the slice you've cut off through the pasta machine on PM3, short end first so it becomes longer. I've done this with the bottom two slices. As you can see, one is longer than the other, so I obviously cut that one slightly thicker. By putting the slices through the pasta machine it means that it doesn't matter if your slices are the same width or not. Lay two slices together as shown, and bunish well with the deli wrap/white paper and soap stone, or whatever you're using to burnish.

Cut the clay to the length needed to wrap around the cat at the widest part of the body.

4

Burnish well to adhere the slices, otherwise when you put them on the cat they will split.

5

With a needle, I've used a 2mm needle, drag it down across the stripes at 5mm intervals.

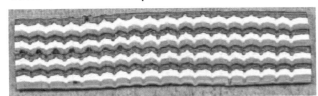

Then turn it over and drag the needle down between the gaps.

6

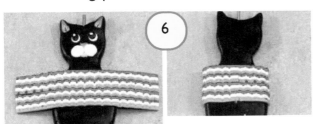

Lay the stripy strip on the front of the cat where you want it to go, then fold round the cat, keeping it straight, cut to size and push the join together.

7

For the jumper ribbing, roll some white clay on PM3 and cut a 3mm strip. Make marks at even intervals all the way along the strip.

8

Gently press the two top edges until they meet the neck. this gives a more realistic jumper effect (if of course you can get your head around cats wearing jumpers in the first place!!)

9

Place the ribbing all round at the top and bottom of the jumper.

To make the arms, roll some clay, the colour of the cat, to a log 5cm long, and 7mm diameter; round each end. Put some jumper clay in the middle, 1.5cm wide, then add ribbing either end.

10

Cut the arms in half, then make three indentation in the 'paw' end of each using your needle tool. Turn each arm over and cut a wedge shape piece out of the under-side, cutting from an angle near the ribbing to the end. This makes it easier to fix the arm to the main cat body.

11

Fix the arms to the top of each side of the jumper as shown.
Finally put the two back feet on, and then cure for 1 hour in a pre-heated over at the clay manufacturers recommended temperature.
For Premo 1 cure at 130°C

and cover the clay in the over. Cure the tail at the same time, and add any extras eg hat, scarf, present, pudding etc before curing your cat.

Making the scarf & hat:

Make a sheet of stripes, but this time with the stripes vertical. Burnish well and cut a thin strip. Put this round the cat's neck, and add an extra piece as shown. Finally make four little cuts in the end to look like scarf tassels

For the hat, roll a small ball of scrap clay, around 1cm diameter, and cover with red clay. Make it into a hat shape and fit onto the top of the head; push the bead pin through the hat.

Add a strip of white clay round the bottom of the hat and texture it with your needle tool or a small ball tool.

Making a Christmas pudding:

Take odd bits of clay in the colours you want the pudding to be. Add a little red, green, and gold

Chop all the clay up with your clay blade, quite finely.

Push the bits of chopped clay into a ball. Then slice it, and chop again, making smaller pieces.

Once you have the clay chopped fine enough, push it into a square block. It's now ready to use to make your pudding.

Roll some scrap clay on PM0 and cut out a 4cm circle. Roll it into a ball and cover in thin slices of the pudding cane, then roll smooth. Cut the pudding ball in half, this will make two puddings.

To make the cream, roll some white clay on PM4 and lay one half of the pudding on top. Cut round half the ball, around 6mm larger, and across the middle. Take off the pudding and with a craft knife cut a wavy line to look like dripping cream. Finally gently put the cream on the pudding.

You're going to make the leaf in a similar way to the pudding. Take some various shades of green and chop them finely.

Push the clay together and roll flat with your clay roller.

When flat enough to put through the pasta machine, put through on PM0. PM2 and PM4. Then roll the clay into a log.

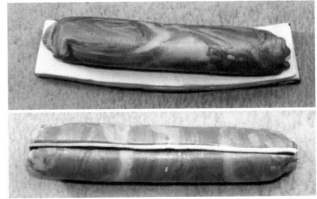

Roll some white, yellow and black clay on PM4 about the size of the log. Stack it and put through the pasta machine on PM0, PM1, PM3 & PM5.

Cut the log in half lengthways, cover one half with a piece of the white/yellow/black clay, and put the two halves back together. Lengthen the cane to the size of leaf you need.

on PM5 and lay the nail foil on top. If the foil curls, put the curled side on the clay, but don't worry, because if you put it the wrong way up it won't hurt it, it will still work when you turn it over.

Cover the clay and foil with deli wrap or layout paper, and burnish well.

Pinch the cane at each end of the strip to make a leaf shape. Cut a slice off, and using a small circle cutter, cut little 'bites' out of the leaf all the way round. This makes it look like holly.

Make three leaves and put them on top of the pudding. Finally roll three small balls of red clay for the berries.

Making the presents:

For the wrapping paper I've used nail art transfer foils. They're quite cheap on ebay, and are great for things like this. Roll out some clay

To take the foil off, carefully lift one corner then rip it off quickly. It's more likely to come away cleanly if you do this fast. 'Wrap' the paper round scrap clay in the desired shape and add ribbon and a label.

Black & white cats:

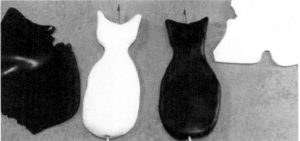

For the black and white cats, I start off with a totally black or totally white cat. Roll some black and white on PM5. You can see that I want my black cat to have a particular shape of white so I've cut it out in readiness.

For the white cat I've cut out circles of clay, and blended them on with a large knitting needle, this smoothes the join and makes the circles look more natural.

On the cat on the right the curved white part on the head was cut out, but the front white patch was torn clay. For this cat I've used my needle tool to make little lines from the white into the black; this gives a more hairy look. Then on the head I've smoothed it with a large knitting needle, and on the patch I've left it without being smoothed so you can see the difference.

Tabby cats:

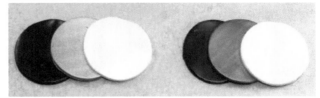

I'm going to make two colours of tabby cat, a silver tabby and a normal brown tabby. For each one roll 3 x 4cm circles of clay on PM0. For the silver tabby I've used black, silver and pearl, and for the brown tabby I've used black, bronze and pearl. Lay them half overlapping as shown.

Put the three overlapping circles through the pasta machine on PM0, with the black one side, pearl the other.

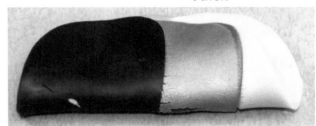

Fold the clay in half, keep the black on one side and pearl the other, and put through the pasta machine again. Keep folding and putting through until you have a blend. I like to keep turning the clay round, so the black is on the right, then the left, then the right etc, but always with the dark one side and the light the other.

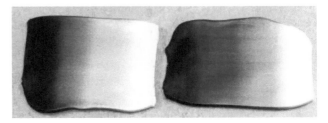

Once you're happy with your blend, fold the clay in half again, as you did for making the blend (picture on the left), then put the folded clay through the pasta machine, but this time with the short end first. Put through on PM0, then PM2, PM4 and PM6. You will end up with a long thin blend (picture on the right).

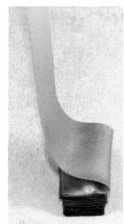

You're now going to make what's called a 'fan fold'. Fold the clay back and forth in 1cm folds. It doesn't matter which end you start as you will finish up with a blended stack of clay. Don't worry if it's not perfect, it's going to be stripes on a cat, and uneven is more natural looking.

Once you have your blend (on the left), roll it with your clay roller until it measures 7cm long (right).

Now put the clay through the pasta machine, short end first, on PM0, you will end up with a longer blend, with light on one side and dark on the other (top picture). Fold it over with the dark clay on the inside (bottom picture).

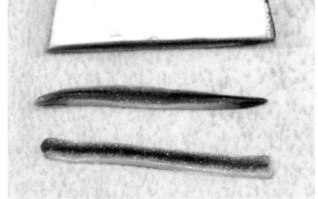

Put it through the pasta machine on PM0 again, short end first, then pinch the two long edges. If you don't do this your slices will have blunt edges, like the slice on the bottom of the picture. By pinching them your slice will have more natural pointy ends.

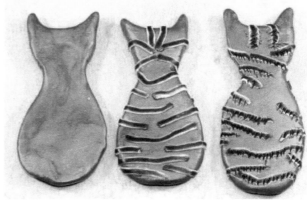

Make your cat base using whatever colour you like, I've used bronze.

Cut thin slices off your cane and put them all over the cat. You can then either use a large knitting needle to blend the stripes onto the cat, and leave it like that, or make it hairier.

To make a hairy cat, use your needle tool and drag it in short lines from the middle of the stripes into the brown clay. Don't make a long line through the whole stripe, do one side - as shown above - then do the other side.

To finish, make short little lines with your needle tool all over the rest of the cat.

Ginger cats:

I've made four types of ginger cats. The one on the left is made by having a plain ginger body, and putting stripes all over it. The stripes are made exactly the same way as for the tabby cats, using black, orange and pearl clay.

However, when you make the fan fold, don't use all the black. Start with the light end, and as soon as the clay becomes black, do a couple of fold maximum, then cut off the rest of the black. It makes it too dark in the middle if you use all the black.

For the cat second from the left I've used the stripes, but also rolled some light orange clay on PM5 and torn little pieces off, placing them on the cat and blending with a large knitting needle.

For the third cat I've done exactly the same but made it hairy, the same as I did for the tabby cats.

For the cat on the right I make a blend as shown below.

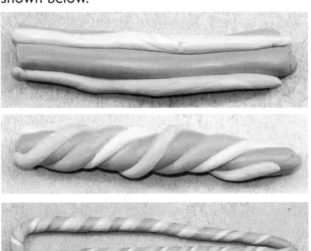

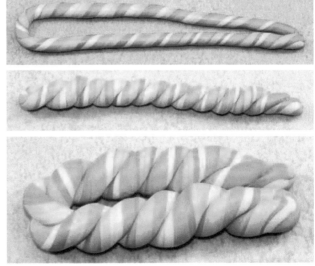

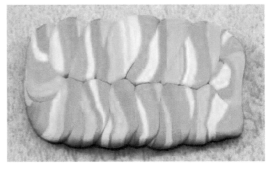

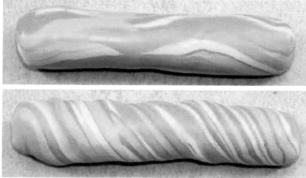

Take some orange clay logs of different shades and twist them together. Roll the log until it's about 3-4 times longer, and twist again.
Fold it in half, and twist again. Fold in half again, then flatten. Put though the pasta machine on PM0, then PM1 and PM3.

Cover a log ready to make into the cat, then you can either make the cat as is, or you can do what I did and twist it again, which gave me the cat on the right in the picture.

Tortoiseshell cat:

I love this cat, and don't think I'm going to be able to sell her! Anyway, to make her, I got different colours of clay, some bronze, various shades of orange, and pearl. Chop them up as you did for the xmas pudding and leaf cane.

Only chop the clay up once, and roll it with your clay roller. Don't worry if there appears to be quite large blocks of colour.

Put it through the pasta machine on PM1 and PM3, then cover the scrap clay to make a body. The top picture has just been covered, the one underneath has been twisted. You can choose to twist or not to twist, twisted gives you more stripes of colour, but untwisted may look just as lovely.

Every one of these cats will be unique.

Grumpy cat in tree lights:

Roll some white clay on PM6 and cut a 6mm circle. Also on PM6 roll some black clay and cut a 4mm circle; place on top of the white circle and cut in half.

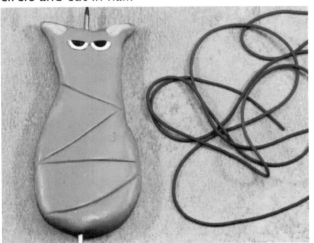

Place the two half circles on the cat for eyes.

For the ears, make them point to the side and slightly downwards; this adds to the discontented look!

For the tree light wire I used a clay extruder and extruded some brown clay on the smallest circle. However, you don't need an extruder, you can just roll very thin logs of clay instead.

With your needle tool make fairly deep lines where you want the clay wire to go in. This makes it easier to have nice straight lines rather than wobbly ones.

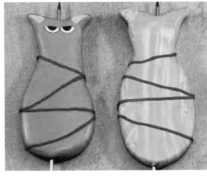

Wrap the clay round the cat and press down gently to adhere. Make sure you have it round the back as well, as Christmas tree decorations don't always stay facing forwards, so it's nice to have an interesting back.

For the lights I use a 3/16" (5mm approx) teardrop cutter, but you can use small circle cutters as well. Roll some different clay colours on PM5. For the silver and gold I've used gold and silver leaf, and the red clay has ultra fine red glitter on it. Cut several of each colour.

Place the lights along the wire, including the back and press gently. For the face use your needle tool to make a slanted mouth, and I've put some whiskers in at the same time as they're all going to be black.

Cure you cats for one hour at the clay manufacturer's recommended temperature, then when cool, back fill the mouth and whisker holes. Do this by pushing clay into the mouth etc, then scrap off the excess and use a wet wipe or cloth to remove any little bits left. Cure for another 5 minutes.

Once cool, use your needle tool and scrap three whiskers either side of the mouth. Back fill as before and cure for another 5 minutes. Your cat is now ready for threading.

Threading your cats:

First you're going to put the eye screw in the top of the tail. For this you need the tail and eye screw, a hand drill with a 1mm drill end, and some superglue. I like using brush-on superglue as it is easier to use on small items.

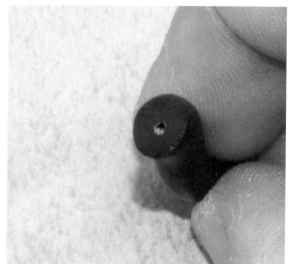

Hold the tail firmly and drill in the flat end, you only have to drill a small way in.

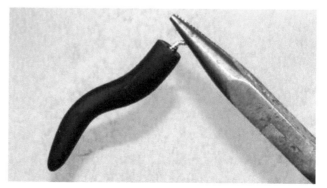

Grasp the eye screw with your pliers, put some superglue on the end of the eye screw and screw it into the tail.

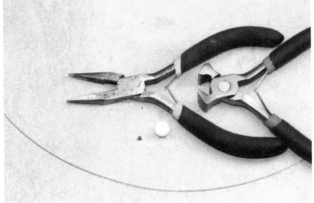

I use Tiger Tail beading wire, and cut a piece 35cm long. You will also need a crimp, and for the cat I'm threading I'm using a white bead for the top of the hat. You may want to use several beads to make a decorative hanging thread, it's totally up to you how decorated you want it.

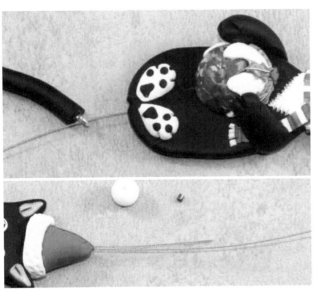

Thread the tiger tail through the top of the cat down to the end, then through the eye screw on the tail and back up to the head end.

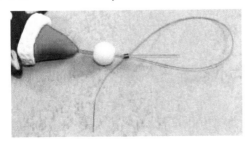

Leave enough thread one end to take whatever beads you're going to use, the longer piece will be making the loop.

Thread the beads and a crimp onto the two threads, then fold the long one back and also thread through the crimp.

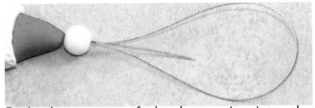

Push the excess of the loop wire into the beads, and with pliars close the crimp by squeezing it flat. Cut the little piece of wire in the middle off just above the crimp.

For the cat with the 7mm rings on the head and tail end, open the eye pin with the pliers, hook it through the 7mm ring and close.

For the head end cut a piece of threading wire around 16cm, thread through the top ring and finish as you did for the other cat.

Casper says he hopes you enjoy making lots and lots of cats!

Suppliers:

Not an extensive list, but the ones that I use.

ClayAround
www.clayaround.com

A real treasure trove of clay goodies for all your claying needs, with exceptional customer service from Penny Vingoe. Categories include:

- Accessories
- Bezel settings
- Clay cutting blades
- Decorating surfaces
- Embossing & distressing
- Fat Daddio cutters
- Gilders wax
- Inka Gold
- Kemper cutters
- Liquid & special clay
- Mica powder
- Pan pastels
- Premo clay
- Souffle clay
- Alcohol inks
- Books
- Crafting tools
- Fimo Clay
- Foils
- Heat set paints
- Kato clay
- Kor tools
- Melanie Muir designs
- Moulds
- Pardo clay
- Silk screens
- Texture makers

Penny keeps up to date with the latest polymer clay tools, materials, products and accessories and sources them from all over the world. ClayAround only ships to the UK and EU.

The Clay Hub:
Premium craft products
www.theclayhub.co.uk

The Clayhub is a Polymer Clay supplier based in the UK. They primarily sell Cernit, but also sell a wide array of accessories, as well as hosting polymer clay workshops in the UK that you can sign up for. The Clayhub is run by a real polymer clay artist with years of experience, and pride themselves on the knowledge they have and good customer service they provide.

Resources:

ClayAround Newsletter

On the ClayAround website you can find a link to sign up for the ClayAround newsletter; Penny puts together a selection of videos and links around a particular clay technique or interest each month, and also features polymer clay artists. A really interesting and informative read.

The British Polymer Clay Guild

A non-profit organisation based in the UK, for members who are interested in learning and sharing tips and techniques about creating art in polymer clay. It's open to all levels of experience, from beginners to professionals, and members include miniaturists, jewellry makers, sculptors, doll makers and anyone interested in polymer clay. It's a really supportive and informative group, and one I recommend everyone joins.

The Blue Bottle Tree
https://thebluebottletree.com

Ginger Davis Allman is the face behind this incredibly useful site. Ginger researches many tools and products associated with polymer clay and writes reports on them so you can make an informed choice. On her site you can find:

- Articles useful for the polymer clay beginner
- Polymer clay tutorials to purchase - knowledge and techniques
- Free polymer clay articles, covering a wide range of techniques, product information, and guidelines
- Sign up to get more free polymer clay information, tips, and offers in your email.

Glossary:

Several times I've been asked what I mean by a word; I've put together a few of the words that might need some further explanation.

Acrylic or metal clay roller:
An acrylic or metal rolling pin for rolling clay into a sheet. If you don't have one of these, a glass jar or bottle can work well.

Ball tool:
A tool with a ball on one or both ends, which can be used in a variety of ways including making texture, adding contours and definition, or smoothing over two clay joins.

Bulls eye cane:
A cane wrapped in a sheet of clay in another colour, or several sheets of colour.

Cane:
A tube of clay, with a pattern that goes all the way along, like a stick of seaside rock. Slices are taken off the cane and used in a variety of ways.

Conditioning:
When clay is in its packet, the various components of the clay can separate. Conditioning is working the clay until it is pliable and does not crack when folded. Not conditioning clay can result in weaker clay that is likely to break easily or crack once cured.

Curing:
Curing is the same as baking, and can be done in a normal oven. Ginger Davis Allman from The Blue Bottle Tree gives a good explanation:

"Polymer clay is PVC powder mixed with plasticizer and some other stuff (fillers, binders, pigment, etc). And as the heat in the oven rises, the PVC particles swell up a bit and soften, eventually fusing into a solid mass that we know as cured polymer clay".

Clay extruder, or Clay gun:
A tool that can create long lengths of clay in a uniformed shape.

Log:
A length of rolled clay, also called a 'snake'.

Mica powder:
Finely ground mica particles that are dyed. When applied to un-cured clay they give a metalic sheen.

Needle tool:
A tool with a long pointed tip which can be used to make bead holes or texture.

Polymer clay:
A type of modelling clay that is primarily polyvinyl chloride (PVC), a plastic. It can be shaped and re-shaped, and needs to be cured (baked) at a low temperature in a normal oven in order to become hard and durable.

Polymer clay adhesive:
There are various types of this, I use Bake & Bond mostly. Polymer clay adhesive can be applied to clay and it will bond cured and non-cured clay when baked.

Skinner blend:
A method of blending two or more colours to make a sheet of smoothly graduated coloured clay. It was developed by Judith Skinner in 1996 and is the basis for most canes.

Tissue blade:
An extremely sharp blade used for cutting and slicing polymer clay; the blades can be flexible, rigid or wavy.

CPSIA information can be obtained
at www.ICGtesting.com
Printed in the USA
BVHW021748091221
623626BV00002B/13